GW00467583

THE

German Shepherd Dog
(Alsatian) Owner's
ENCYCLOPAEDIA

MADELEINE PICKUP

PELHAM BOOKS

By the same author
ALL ABOUT THE GERMAN SHEPHERD DOG

First published in Great Britain by
PELHAM BOOKS LTD
44 Bedford Square
London, WC1B 3DU
JUNE 1964

SECOND IMPRESSION SEPTEMBER 1965
THIRD IMPRESSION MARCH 1967
FOURTH IMPRESSION JUNE 1968
FIFTH IMPRESSION DECEMBER 1969
SIXTH IMPRESSION JULY 1971
SEVENTH IMPRESSION NOVEMBER 1974
EIGHTH IMPRESSION MAY 1977

SECOND EDITION 1981

ISBN 0 7207 1300 5

Printed in Great Britain by Hollen Street Press, Slough,
and bound by Redwood Burn Ltd., Esher

DEDICATION

To The Lady Kitty Ritson (*née* Ogilvy, of the
Bonnie House of Airlie) who has shone ahead
'blade straight and steel true', since the early
thirties when I first fell in love with Donald of
Tulchan, to teach me with her gay and ever-
youthful outlook that dog-breeding can be fun,
even to the dedicated; and that among German
Shepherd fanciers are those as steadfast and
devoted in friendship as are our beloved breed
to their owners.

FOREWORD

It gives me much pleasure to write this foreword to *The German Shepherd Dog (Alsatian) Owner's Encyclopaedia*. Nothing could be more valuable to newcomers to the breed, and to novices, than advice from someone like Mrs Pickup who has gained her experience the hard way, that is, by starting at the bottom and climbing to the top. Mrs Pickup has always written to give help and information to those who wish to be successful with their dogs in the show ring or as family companions.

I feel sure that this Encyclopaedia about the German Shepherd Dog will fill a long-felt want, bringing others the same enjoyment from the breed as it has to the authoress, who has overcome all difficulties to achieve success.

James Y. Baldwin

Abbreviations: The letters placed after a dog's name on pedigree or show catalogue are the training degrees won in either obedience tests or working trials. The following are the German titles with their English translation:

AD	Ausdauer — Passed Endurance Test
BPDH I, II	Bahnpolizeidiensthund — Railway Police Dog
BDH†	Bahndiensthund — Railway Service Dog
BlH	Blindenführhund — Guide Dog for Blind
DH	Diensthund — Working Dog in a Service
DPH	Dienstpolizeihund — Service Police Dog
FH	Fahrtenhund — Field trials Tracking Dog
HGH	Herdengebrauchshund — Herding Dog
Int. Pr. Kl.	Internationale Prüfungsklasse — International Trials Class
Kr.H†	Kriegshund — War Dog
K.Sch.H†	Kriegsschutzhund — War Defence Dog or Guard Dog
LS†	Leistungsieger — Field Trial Champion
MH I, II	Meldehund — Messenger Dog
PFP I, II	Polizeifährtenhundprüfung — Police tracking-dog Test
PH	Polizeihund — Police Dog
PHD†	Polizeidiensthund — Police Dog on Patrol Service
PSP I, II	Polizeischutzhund-Prüfung — Police Guard Dog Test
SH I, II	Sanitätshund — Red Cross Dog
SchH I, II, III	Schutzhund — Guard or Defence Dog
SuchH†	Suchhund — Tracking Dog
ZH I, II	Zollhund — Customs Dog
ZFH	Zollfährtenhund — Customs tracker dog
ZPr	Zuchtprüfung bestanden — passed temperament test for breeding

Titles marked † are no longer in use, but still appear on many pedigrees, as they were current when bestowed on the dogs against whose names they appear.

The following are the purely English degrees:

C.D.	Companion Dog
P.D.	Police Dog
T.D.	Tracking Dog
U.D.	Utility Dog
W.D.	Working Dog (another version of U.D.)
W.T.Ch.	Working Trials Champion

Note: Any of the English working degrees can carry (Ex.) – 'excellent' – which denotes an especially high standard of work (80% marks or better).

Acetabulum Dysplasia (or Hip Dysplasia): This has been the subject of great controversy on both sides of the Atlantic. It is generally recognised as an abnormally shallow hip-bone socket (or acetabulum) which affects the hind action and if present to any degree can cause pain when the dog jumps or moves over uneven ground. In advanced stages, the actual click as the bone slips in and out of the socket can be audibly discerned.

There is at present no veterinary ruling on the theory that the disease is hereditary. It has been said that it is caused by a deficient diet or from muscular sources due to lack of exercise. It should be considered on the same level as any other unsoundness when making plans for breeding. There is neither cure nor remedy, and usually the condition remains unchanged with age, many dogs living a happy, if somewhat restricted life with the affliction, if it is not too severe.

Action (otherwise 'Gait' or 'Movement'): This is one of the most important points in a German Shepherd. All the various points in his construction culminate in his action, and he is assessed largely on this, particularly in his country of origin – not only on the soundness thereof but on the elasticity of his step and the endurance of the trot for long periods. The German Shepherd is not naturally a fast gaiting dog: his normal average speed is about 4 m.p.h., the brisk walking pace of a man in fact, which gives weight to the writer's contention that the dog should always be shown on a loose lead and not hauled round the ring on a tightly-held slip chain. Swift movement can disguise faults, and a dog will present a true picture of himself only if he is allowed to set the pace. Our best handlers adjust their speed to suit the individual dog, and to see them moving as one is a real pleasure. 'Weaving' or 'plaiting' of the feet, either front or rear, is a sign of weakness or unsoundness, and should be penalised if displayed continually in action. A dog occasionally crosses his feet when travelling over rough ground or changing his direction, and this should be taken into account. A dog of this breed moving soundly at his natural speed is one of the most beautiful sights at any dog show.

Aggressiveness: In common with other breeds there are some G.S.D.s which develop this unfortunate characteristic. It can be highly dangerous in such a large breed, and if possible the source or cause should be investigated and eradicated. Failing this, the dog's instincts should be guided into other channels either by having him trained or, better still, taking him to training classes, where he will learn to take his proper place in society and have an outlet for his intelligence. Frustration is often the root cause of aggression, and a dog with his mind on pleasing his master is not usually afflicted with this most undesirable fault.

Albino (*see also* STANDARD and COLOUR): White coats with pink or discoloured noses, and claws white or yellow, are not in the standard; and if the breeder is unwilling to have them put down at birth they should be given away without pedigrees as pets only, and spayed to prevent reproduction. Lack of pigmentation is a serious fault; all pale colours are undesirable; and white is not admitted by the breed standard.

Alsatian (Origin of the Name): Our dog was introduced into this country at the end of World War I, when everything German was extremely unpopular: even the harmless little Dachshund had been stoned by zealous patriots during the years of combat. It was considered that the breed would get off to a bad start if the correct name was used, so it became the Alsatian Wolf Dog, as a kind of translation of Berger d'Alsace (Alsatian Shepherd), giving both France and Germany the benefit of the doubt! In the 1930s the Kennel Club granted permission to put '(German Shepherd Dog)' after 'Alsatian', but this seemed both long-winded and inconvenient. With the enlightened outlook of breeders after World War II, pressure was increased to have the name changed to the correct one. Finally, in 1977, the Kennel Club yielded to the majority opinion, and our dog became known as 'German Shepherd Dog (Alsatian)', the last part seldom being used, so that we now conform with the rest of the world. This is a matter of satisfaction for British breeders, particularly in international and export dealings.

Alsatian League, now German Shepherd Dog League of Great Britain or "The League": This is the original Breed Club founded in 1919, one of the founder members being Air Commodore J.A.C. Cecil Wright, A.F.C., T.D., D.L., A.E., who is still active as the President although well into his nineties. The League runs two Open Shows, one in Spring and the second in the Autumn, with an especially fine Championship event in midsummer, which is the highlight of the breed's Show Calendar. Lectures, teach-ins and social events are held frequently, and draw an attendance from many areas. The strongly representative elective Council meets every few weeks to deal with all enquiries and matters relating to the Breed. Many smaller Clubs are affiliated to the League, which supports Shows held all over the British Isles and overseas. Members benefit from a good Comprehensive Insurance scheme; and special facilities for legal advice. Help and guidance on all breed matters are willingly given to all members. The "League Magazine", published quarterly, is available to non-members, as is the handbook published every alternate year. The Hon. Secretary is Mrs J. Ixer, Whitmore Vale End, Hindhead, Surrey GU26 6JB, (tel: Headley Down 3314).

Ambling (or Pacing): This is a fault in movement in the show ring; but like the jog-trot in horses, dogs appear to find it a very comfortable manner of getting about, particularly when tired or overheated. It certainly is not graceful, and can spoil a dog's chances of winning, and therefore it should be discouraged and corrected if possible. If the dog is pushed behind the handler and then drawn forward it will usually break the 'amble'. Another way is to encourage the dog to leap upwards by attracting his attention, and using the opportunity to break the 'amble' much in the same way one changes a leg when riding horseback.

America (German Shepherd Dog Club of): This is the parent Club, operating in the same way as the S.V. (the parent Club in the country of origin) operates in Germany. It is a powerful governing body with nation-wide branches all controlled by the same set of rules and dependent on headquarters for ruling and guidance. The Club's National Show is held in a different area each year, and the regional Club acts as host and organiser. The whole affair is splendidly done with great enthusiasm and pride in the achievement, and at this show the Grand Victor and Grand Victrix are selected. The Club issues a monthly review which is full of interesting articles with photographs of most of the important winners on beautiful quality paper. The Editor is Mrs T.L. Bennett, P.O. Box 1221, Lancaster, Pa., U.S.A.

Angekört: This is the official certificate of the S.V. that the animal has been submitted to a Breed Survey (Körung) and approved for breeding. It is denoted by an 'x' in a German Show catalogue.

Angulation: This is the slope or angle of the shoulder-blade in the forequarters and the sharp angles of the inter-related bones in the hindquarters — thigh, hock and metatarsus. The balance of the dog depends very much on the harmony of its angulation at both ends. The thigh bone should ideally parallel the shoulder-blade, with the stifle bone paralleling the upper arm. Any extreme or exaggerated angles are faults not only of balance but because they denote weakness possibly of bone texture, and give an over-elegant appearance not typical of a working dog.

Appetite (*see also* FOOD and DIET): As a rule a properly exercised dog will always eat heartily, and as the Shepherd Dog is designed to work and cover miles over rough ground at his job it must be recognised that he needs plenty of exercise to keep him in condition — so the first necessity for a good appetite is sufficient exercise. The second is a clean and regular intestine, and this is dependent on the above as well as on his diet. A dog recovering from illness or a change of environment may need tempting a little to get him to eat — keep the meals small at first, in this case, and try to find out what preferences he has and use these to coax him to eat. Sometimes a little grated cheese sprinkled over the bowl will help, or some liver, boiled, then cut into squares the size of sugar lumps and baked in the oven until very firm. A dozen or so of these cubes mixed into the food will stimulate appetite. Some dogs like sardines, and as these are very nourishing they are useful additions to a convalescent dog's diet — two or three with some of the oil make a tasty supplement to any meal.

In hot weather it is wise to cut down the quantity of all food, particularly starches. Give a tablespoon of grated raw carrot or a little finely-chopped watercress in the main meal and plenty of fresh garlic. Naturally, in cold weather the rations should be increased, some extra warming foods being included such as a tablespoonful of finely-grated suet or a herring, prepared by cutting off the head, boiling for five minutes, and removing the backbone and sharp fins — the fine bones are harmless. A good drink of milk and honey at night will keep a dog warm in his kennel — just melt a dessertspoonful of honey in warm water and add luke-warm milk: cooking honey destroys the vitamins.

Appetite, depraved: This distressing habit does not seem to follow any pattern. It is thought to denote a lack of minerals or vitamins in the food, or an irritation in the stomach. The unclean habit of devouring excreta is sometimes an indication that a bitch is in whelp and is reverting to the wild animal's instinct to cover her tracks. A dose of milk of magnesia (a tablespoonful for an adult) will sometimes help clear up the trouble if it is caused by indigestion; and the dog should be supervised at exercise and the faeces removed before he can devour them. In puppies, teething can cause this unpleasant tendency, and a small dose of milk of magnesia for a day or two is usually enough to put matters right.

Approach: Most sheep or herding breeds dislike being handled by strangers, despite the fact that they can be trained to accept this as part of the procedure in the show ring. It is decidedly against their true instincts and many with otherwise firm character will retreat from intimate handling. It must be remembered that the breed has great natural dignity, clearly shown in its noble outlook; and just as we humans would resent a familiar greeting from a stranger, so do they— and in dealing with them this should be borne in mind. Walk up to the dog quietly, speak to him and watch his eyes: if his character is average he will doubtless look indifferent or even inattentive to your overtures, or dismiss you with a brief wag of the tail and a keen glance. This should be accepted as a normal reaction to the proper approach in an intelligent and discerning animal. Hasty and fussy approach will alarm and upset a dog which is quite firm in character but intolerant of human excesses.

A.S.P.A.D.S.: The doyen of our Training Clubs, which came into being at a Kennel Club show at the old Crystal Palace in 1921. Capt. Redcliffe and Mrs M.E. Griffin were the prime movers, the latter becoming secretary. The original Committee consisted of Col. J.Y. Baldwin, Major Budd, Mr Lionel de Pinto and Mrs Veitch.

The main object of the Society was to train dogs of all breeds, and its original name was The Alsatian, Sheep, Police and Army Dogs Society. Afterwards, Mrs Griffin went to New Zealand, where she used Alsatians for sheep herding with great and recognised success; and the Society subsequently became known by its present title of the Associated Sheep, Police and Army Dogs Society.

The Society holds trials throughout the year but none for sheep herding at present, although this continues, with dogs of Mrs Griffin's old Hettel Uckermark strain: one descendent, Crumstone Lance, has worked all kinds of stock on Mr Ronald Smith's estate at Stoke Talmage; he records that he has never lost an animal since Lance took over.

Ausdauer: The Ausdauer Prüfung causes much interest in Great Britain as we have no test remotely resembling it. Briefly, the adult dog has to run beside a bicycle for 20 kilometres, with halts at certain stages to ascertain that his feet are not damaged or causing him pain, when he would be instantly withdrawn. At the end of the 20 kilometres, after a brief pause, he must do some simple obedience tests to show that he has not been mentally affected by the long run. He is examined by veterinary surgeons and senior S.V. officials, his heart and lungs are tested and his feet carefully scrutinised, and his temperament reassessed, since, as we have pointed out, physical beauty and even toughness are considered by the Germans only when the dog has the correct German Shepherd character. One could say that a dog which comes through such a gruelling test is indeed worthy of his name.

Bad Breath: This can be caused by defective teeth, so have them examined by your Veterinary Surgeon if you are in doubt. Worms are another cause, and the faeces should be examined for segments of tapeworms or the presence of the round variety. For a temporary attack of this unpleasant malady, during recovery from an illness perhaps, a few doses of Amplex tablets, and rubbing the teeth with a clean piece of damp linen dipped in bicarbonate of soda will help.

B.A.G.S.D. British Association for German Shepherd Dogs: First formed in 1930 under its original title of Birmingham and District Alsatian Club, the founder and chairman being Mr F. Riego, who continues to occupy that office, and also that of president. The Club started with about 100 members; and when membership increased to around 1,000 with many branches in the Midlands, its name was changed to Midland Alsatian Association. After World War II Mr Riego started to build up the Club into a national one, for which the Kennel Club eventually granted the title British Alsatian Association, under which name branches were formed throughout the country. Then, when the breed's correct name was officially assumed in 1977, the present title was adopted. The B.A.G.S.D. has some 60 branches, each one holding training classes for obedience and handling in the show ring. A fine Breed Championship Show, usually with top foreign judges, is held every summer; and schools have been opened to produce qualified obedience trainers. Two Open Shows are held each year, one in London and the other in Scotland, with a 3 days' Working Trials event usually staged in the Midlands in September. Headquarters are at 55a South Road, Erdington, Birmingham 23.

Ball-playing: All dogs delight in playing with a ball, but this should be allowed only under strict supervision. See that the ball is large enough (*not* tennis size for adults) or it may be swallowed, or become lodged in the throat and cause asphyxiation. Soft balls are also dangerous, as the strong teeth may rip off small pieces, and if swallowed these may have severe reactions.

Barking: Unnecessary and repeated barking can be a source of much annoyance to owners and neighbours, and should be firmly checked in puppyhood by a light tap with a rolled-up newspaper and a firm voice saying 'No—Blank—No!' Blank for the dog's name, always coupled with the command. It is as well to ascertain whether the dog is cold or wants to be exercised, of course, before reproving him. (*See also* BOREDOM).

Bathing (*see* CLEANLINESS).

Bedding: German Shepherds do not suffer from the cold if they have the correct coat (*see* COAT); but they cannot tolerate draughts or damp sleeping quarters, and if they are to be free from rheumatic diseases every effort should be made to bed them down suitably. One of the proprietory makes of canvas dog beds is excellent, or a wooden bench on low legs to raise it about 9 inches off the floor, covered with a couple of clean sacks (we wash ours each week in a weak solution of Dettol). Naturally, a dog should sleep in a temperature similar to that in which he lives in the daytime. It would be both cruel and stupid, for example, to put him out to sleep in an unheated kennel if he spends his evenings by the fireside or in a centrally-heated house. He has good resistance to cold if he is kept outside always, however, and is quite happy in a draught-free kennel with a raised bench and plenty of wood-wool, or some sacks lightly stuffed with it, if you dislike the mess it makes, to keep him cosy. Straw is undesirable as bedding: it smells musty and frequently contains insects; also, sharp pieces can injure the dog's eyes and nostrils, particularly in puppyhood.

Begging: Everyone likes to reward a dog with tit-bits; but a dog which begs at table is an embarrassment and a nuisance. Never give food from the table, and a dog will neither expect nor request it. Our own house-dogs always queue-up in the kitchen after meals for any small suitable left-overs or a morsel of cheese — which satisfies our desire for indulging them and their own polite inquiring sniffs when there is something particularly savoury on the table.

Belly Mantle: The thick, soft hair covering the underbelly of the dog, heavier in winter, and soft and profuse in bitches who shed most of it when nearing motherhood.

Biscuits (or biscuit meal): Only first quality wholemeal biscuit or rusk is suitable, as Shepherds overheat easily and many skin and digestive maladies are due to feeding white or agenised flour products. Biscuits containing dried or dehydrated meat are also most unsuitable. Best of all is the home-made rusk, made from cutting wholemeal bread into cubes and drying (not toasting) them in a cool oven or on top of the hot water tank.

Bleeding: Any sign of loss of blood should be investigated thoroughly and immediately; and if no cuts or other outward signs are visible of a nature which can be dealt with from the animal medicine chest, then send for your veterinary surgeon at once.

Blistered Feet (*see also* FEET): In a breed that owes so much to movement, feet are of paramount importance, and such a heavy dog makes it difficult to heal any injuries to them. Blisters caused by tarry substances from the roads can be helped by applying butter to soften and remove the tar. Then hold the foot in a jam-jar of water with either a weak solution of Permanganate of Potash or T.C.P.; dry with folded cleansing tissues lightly held on the tender spots; and dust with powdered alum or zinc/boracic. Blisters from unaccustomed roadwork etc. can be tackled the same way, leaving out the butter application.

Blue Colour: Many puppies are born 'blue' in colour; and unless they have other faults it is unwise to put them down for faulty pigmentation, as they frequently change and become normal – either black and tan or golden sable. This blue colour is similar to a blue fox, and is sometimes called 'smoky'. It is not a desirable colour; but if the nose and nails are dark there is no reason to doubt that the puppy will be an acceptable colour when matured.

Bones: Only large, preferably shin bones should be given; always cooked and if possible sawn not chopped, as the small, sharp pieces adhering to a chopped bone can cause an internal haemorrhage.

Boredom: Due to their great intelligence and working ability, Shepherds grow bored with confinement and inactivity; and this boredom can affect their character and disposition. Dogs like routine, and will adjust themselves to their owners' habits; but they love anything in the nature of a surprise outing or some work they can share – shifting logs or 'helping' make a bonfire in the garden, carrying a shopping basket or any of the many tasks within their scope. A short period of daily training keeps them up to the mark, too; and if it is at all possible every dog should attend training classes or be given simple training at home, to exercise his mind and draw out his working-dog characteristics. A bored or lonely dog is usually difficult or badly behaved, so give him plenty of attention and outlet for his wonderful intelligence.

Breeding: We consider it a general rule that a bitch in normal health should have at least two litters in her lifetime—the first one at her third heat or about two years of age. Our breed has so much growth and development to achieve in youth that a young bitch has nothing to spare to give her puppies before this age, and both dam and litter would suffer if she mated earlier. It is quite a good plan, if frequent litters are not desired, to let her have her second family at six years, so that she is ready for a healthy old age. On *no* account should a bitch be bred from more than once yearly, or every second heat. Shepherds are usually easy whelpers and excellent mothers; but huge quantities of food and plenty of space for the rapidly growing youngsters are necessary, so that only those with serious intentions should undertake this delightful task. 'Pet' litters are definitely not for this breed, which is expensive to rear and house.

Brushing (*see* GROOMING).

Cat Feet: The rounded, short-toed foot, much prized, is often thus described; and is considered stronger and better in a working breed than the longer or 'hare' foot. This latter, if not exaggerated, is quite acceptable in the standard, the ideal being somewhere between the two.

Calcium Deficiency: In a breed which has to make such a large amount of strong bone, this has become one of our chief concerns, and is largely due to the way our dogs' food is produced in modern times — wheat for their biscuit or rusk from artificially manured fields, meat from chemically treated pastures etc, and to the lack of sunshine so deplorable in our climate.

The best way to counteract this deficiency by normal means is in the diet. Give olive oil of the first quality, starting from a few drops in puppyhood to a large teaspoonful for adults. This is a true sunshine food, and benefits the intestine and coat as well. Finely-shredded raw carrot, again starting with small quantities and working up to a heaped tablespoonful by a year old. We use a grater of the kind used at the famous Bircher Benner Health Clinic, as it shreds the vegetable finely and easily and it cannot thus be 'picked out', although most of our dogs will gnaw carrots like bones. Fresh milk, particularly goats' milk, is excellent, but not dried milk, as this is 'dead' and only provides fats. Pure wheaten semolina boiled as porridge, sweetened with honey and fresh milk, is also another guard against calcium deficiency; and if a few calcium tablets (with Vitamin D) are given over the major periods of growth and to the nursing bitch, there should be no lack of this vital product for a firm frame and strong bone. In severe cases of deficiency, the Veterinary Surgeon will inject calcium intravenously; but sound diet is the best way to prevent this becoming necessary.

Cleanliness: Shepherd Dogs in good health have practically no canine odour and do not normally require bathing. Good and thorough grooming is sufficient (*see* GROOMING) and when the dog comes in wet and dirty he can be cleansed and dried by rubbing with a large wash-leather, well wrung out in warm water repeatedly and used with as much friction as possible. The coat will be dry and gleaming afterwards. If rubber gloves are worn by ladies for this operation, it will be found less messy and troublesome than using a towel, which must be washed afterwards.

The teeth can be cleaned by dipping a soft piece of linen in peroxide of hydrogen and then in a little powdered pumice. Rub gently, avoiding the gums, and sponge the mouth out with clean water on a plastic sponge afterwards. Ears need attention, too, particularly in dry or dusty weather. A piece of cotton wool, wrapped round the index finger and soaked in sweet almond oil, and inserted in the ears will loosen dirt and grease if left for a short time; and then remove with cleansing tissues or cheese muslin. Never use a sharp instrument in a dog's ear, and avoid water, which can cause any foreign body to swell and cause injury and pain. A dog's ear is extremely sensitive, but if the cleansing is done regularly and with patience and gentleness it is usually accepted with the same pleasure as the grooming ritual.

If the dog has rolled in something unpleasant, or must be bathed for some reason, it is best to use Canex soap for shampooing, and to rinse thoroughly with several pails of lukewarm water containing a little 'Dettol', taking care always not to get either solution in the eyes or ears. A thick clean newspaper folded round the body will blot-up much of the moisture; and if possible give a short, brisk walk or run on the lead to stimulate the circulation and avoid a chill.

Character: Nothing is so important in this breed as good, firm character: it has been described as well over 50% of a good Shepherd Dog, a description with which we heartily concur. This is a sensitive breed with quick reactions; and these must be trained for their proper use in the vigilance of the guard dog of home or other property, in the guide dog, or the sheep or farmer's dog. The deep wisdom reflected in the soft, brown eyes of the dog with true Shepherd character is one of the breed's loveliest assets, and possessed only by one with strong nerves trained to accept the noises and vicissitudes of everyday life, and not shut-up for long periods in kennels, where its great intelligence slips back, and loneliness and frustration build up a highly-strung nervous system through lack of familiarity with the outside world.

Shepherd dogs are family dogs, equipped in every way for the task of guarding and defending their masters and those of his household. They should never be kept in large numbers for this reason; and while they can be kennelled comfortably for sleeping, and enjoy free exercise in outdoor paddocks or runs, each one should have some period either indoors or in close human companionship each day, to develop their characters. Here the training classes do fine work; and it is recommended, particularly to novices or those with a 'One and only', to attend these whenever possible.

Claws (or Nails): A dog with a well-muscled foot which has correct exercise will have short, sturdy claws; but sometimes, due to weather conditions or illness the claws become long, which is both ugly and dangerous. It must be remembered that the tender quick also grows, and it is stupid and cruel to attempt to shorten the claws in one clipping; the points only should be removed with heavy nail clippers; and if by any mischance the quick is severed, dab it at once with a swab of cotton-wool soaked in T.C.P. or iodine. It is a very painful accident and should be avoided if possible as it causes the dog to dread this somewhat necessary operation, which may have to be repeated at intervals until the claws are of normal length. It may be advisable to bandage the dog's muzzle during the actual clipping; and two people as experienced and competent as possible should undertake the task. If this is not convenient, take the dog to a Veterinary Surgeon rather than risk the damage which may be caused by clumsy or inexperienced hands.

The claws of nursing puppies should have the tiny white tips snipped regularly from three weeks old onwards during the nursing period, as they cause pain to their dam by tearing her teats and may discourage her from feeding them. This gentle regular attention will also help to get the puppy 'up on his toes' and form a strong foot later.

The dew claws on the hind legs should always be removed by surgery at 3-4 days old when the operation causes the minimum of pain and discomfort. Take care that the dam is shut up out of earshot during the operation, which is perforce best done by your veterinary surgeon.

There is a feeling among some breeders that the claws should be dark in colour, but it has been proved that light coloured claws are not a fault.

Coat: The correct Shepherd Dog coat is not easy to define in terms of touch or handling. It is really a cross between harsh and soft, as the outer coat should be somewhat coarse, and lie straight and flat over the top of the dense, soft undercoat. This undercoat can vary a little in density according to climatic and seasonal conditions; but it is the dog's natural insulation against variations in temperature, as well as a protection against insect pests, and is of great importance if the dog is used for outdoor work. The coat is longer and stronger in growth and density over the throat and neck and behind the flanks — nature's provision for his protection if seized by an enemy at these vital points.

Long coats are faulty by the world-wide accepted standards, and in any case they hide the true beauty of outline and detract from the clean-cut appearance of the typical Shepherd. A slight waviness or curliness is not usually frowned upon, but it is again a question of degree.

Collars: The slip chain in chromium, as fine as possible without weakness, is recommended, as it preserves the ruff of strong hair on the neck, which is one of the great beauties of the breed. It can be pulled tight to correct or control the dog, and worn constantly without chafing the neck. A small, very light one should be put on a young puppy at about three months old for a few minutes each day, to accustom him to the idea, without using the slip chain as a control until he is quite happy to wear it and accepts it as a normal procedure. It is a good plan to remove the slip chain if the dog is running free at exercise in wooded or bush covered country, as he may catch the end loop on a branch, and strangle himself in the effort to get free. (See page 14).

Collie-headed: This is an ugly fault that occurs quite frequently in the breed: the head is too narrow, sometimes in both skull and foreface, particularly the latter; and often this fault carries the additional one of an uneven dentition and overlong upper jaw. It is considered that the fault is produced by badly blending blood-lines of the parents or through over-breeding.

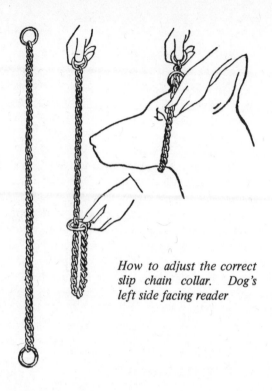

*How to adjust the correct
slip chain collar. Dog's
left side facing reader*

Colour (*see also* STANDARD *and* ALBINO): We are fortunate in our standard, which permits a wide range of colour, the only faulty ones being those showing paling or lack of pigmentation. Black and tan or black and gold are much sought-after, as being 'glamorous' in the show-ring; but many prefer the wide range of sable shades, from iron grey through to golden, all of which are acceptable if the nose and lips, muzzle, too, if possible, are well pigmented and the eye a deep soft brown. All-black is occasionally seen; but a dog without markings must be of very high quality to attract attention, the lovely shading of a Shepherd's coat being one of its great beauties. White is not allowed in the Standard.

Constipation: If only temporary, there are several harmless remedies from the home medicine chest which will ease the situation; but each case must be treated as individual, and the remedy given related to the cause (if known) and the age of the sufferer. When the diet has been restricted in bulk through illness or pregnancy, give a tablespoonful of half liquid paraffin and half pure olive oil every two days until regularity is restored. If the excreta is pale in colour and hard, give a tablespoonful of milk of magnesia, fasting each morning for three days, rest two days, then resume for three days until normal consistency of a well-formed deep brown motion is restored. Ageing dogs benefit from youghort or sour milk as a gentle method of keeping the intestine functioning easily.

Critiques: Some of our leading judges are gifted in making 'word pictures' of the dogs which win under them; and these critiques appear in the Show Reports published in the weekly dog press. If you have not been placed and therefore do not qualify for one of these, it is quite customary to send a S.A.E. to the Judge and ask for the courtesy of a private report. This is willingly given and should be accepted as a true critique of the animal as shown on the day — dogs vary in condition and reaction, so do not be too discouraged unless some serious fault is revealed.

Cryptorchidism (or Cryptorchism): This is a condition in which both testicles are retained in the abdomen or the inguinal canal. In the show ring this is a disqualifying fault, yet the writer cannot see eye to eye with this, as the dog himself is incapable of reproduction yet his litter brothers and sisters or his dam may well carry the fault. It is only fair to point out that the fault, which is manifested in the male, is possibly carried by his female relations; and they should be watched in their breeding programme for further evidence of this defect.

Conditioning: This is taken to mean the preparation for the show ring, although all dogs could benefit from an occasional course.

The well-kept dog whose general health is under constant supervision will not require much in the way of conditioning when the show approaches; but due to illness or a mishap, or because (if a bitch) of being confined owing to her season, it may be necessary to put the future exhibit in hand to bring him or her up to the peak we all like to see in the ring. Give two condition powders fasting in the early morning for three days, rest three days, and start again for three more. Do this twice — fifteen days in all.

Check carefully for any evidence of worms, particularly tapeworm in country dwellers—there is no disgrace in a dog having a tapeworm as the eggs are found everywhere, especially where there are wild rabbits. One of our most inveterate hunters had one each year, and as it was expelled at the first sign of its nasty presence she never lost condition. (*See* WORMS for dosage).

If the dog is of normal weight for his age there is no need to alter his diet, and it is as well to get another breeder to express an opinion on this, as one hardly ever notices if a dog which one sees daily puts on the extra pounds, until he stands with his contemporaries in the ring. But give a heaped tablespoonful of finely chopped parsley and watercress each day, also a few ounces of well-boiled liver or an occasional egg-yolk raw on his main meal.

Increase his road work to improve claws and feet; and if he is soft in muscles try throwing a large ball or a stick up a steep bank or quarry side and persuade him to climb up to retrieve. This is excellent for firming up the body, elbows and pasterns.

Bathing is not usually necessary, but take a pail of warm water and a large wash leather (rubber gloves for ladies) and go all over the dog, rubbing in a rotary movement, a couple of days before the event. In the days following, also before entering the ring, finish his grooming with a dry wash leather to put a sheen on his coat.

A week or so before the show inspect his teeth, if this is not done daily, and remove stains and tartar (*see* TEETH). This gives the mouth time to recover, as it may be sore or sensitive if treatment has been necessary, and the dog will react badly to the inspection of his mouth as a result. Ears must also be attended to carefully (*see* CLEANLINESS); and the fur 'pants' sponged with some mild disinfectant.

Our breed fortunately calls for little show preparation, but a gleaming coat and perfect cleanliness of all orifices is essential and will always help the exhibit to make a good impression on Judge and ringsiders alike.

Deafness: Our breed is not prone to deafness as a rule, nor do they lose their hearing to any marked degree until of a very great age; we have had dogs of 14 years whose hearing was quite normal.

To test a dog for defective hearing, whistle to him or bang his dinner bowl when completely out of sight, and get someone to watch his reaction. Dogs, particularly Shepherds, use their eyes and depend on vibrations through the body, particularly the paws, for 'hearing' or perception, so noise made in their sight may produce a reaction which has not been produced through the ears.

Temporary deafness may be brought about by an ailment such as canker or eczema, or even an insect sting which has become infected.

If the dog rubs his head on the ground or shakes it and carries it on one side, then you may be sure he has an obstruction or ailment in the ear. Examine it gently and smell the inside of the ear, as canker produces a musty, unpleasant smell and any other infection will do likewise inside the cavity. If you think he has an obstruction, gently pour a little slightly warmed sweet almond oil into the ear. This should loosen and float the object, when it can be removed: it will bring out wax and dirt, which can also impair hearing if caked or encrusted by weather or neglect. Always dry a dog's ears after bathing or swimming so that he is not tempted to rub them in the dirt and cause infection or irritation. A thickly folded cleansing tissue is useful, men's size for preference, for this task.

Cleaning an ear calls for a certain amount of skill and aptitude. If you are in doubt, or the sufferer is not co-operative, take him to the veterinary surgeon, as damage once inflicted could cause permanent deafness or injury.

Defence Dogs: No other breed is used so universally as ours for work with the armed forces in peace and war. Ancient carvings, made many years B.C., have been unearthed, showing dogs taking part in battles. These were not Shepherds, of course, but resembled Basenjis or whippets; and this is possibly one of the earliest examples of the dog's services to his master.

The Germans naturally enough were the first Europeans to use the breed to any extent in this field, and had Red Cross and also messenger dogs working in the 1914-18 war. In 1940 they had a four-footed army of many tens of thousands. In England, we used the breed in large numbers with marked success, particularly in the R.A.F., where they excelled in sentry duties: it was said that one man with a dog equalled six men at this work, which was of the highest importance in guarding vital supplies and secret hideaways alike. The Russians also had a canine corps, but we have few details of it. The Swiss army use them chiefly as messenger dogs: in their mountainous country, where field communications are hard to establish, their services are highly valued, also as rescue dogs in avalanches and climbing accidents. Sometimes when on holiday one may notice a Shepherd steadily climbing some steep slope with the tiny cartouche or message-container attached to his collar.

Depraved Appetite (*see* APPETITE, DEPRAVED).

Dew Claws (*see* CLAWS).

Diarrhoea: This symptom that all is not well with the dog varies enormously in significance; but it is a strong hint for the owner to keep a sharp eye on the sufferer. Poisoning and distemper start with it, and the latter with a sharp rise in temperature. So have the thermometer at hand and check at intervals for any sign of fever.

Some dogs, particularly those who have had enteritis or any internal trouble, are very sensitive to a change of diet or even of drinking water. If this is the case, distress can be avoided by taking the dog's normal food with him when he goes to shows or away from home for brief visits, and, if possible, one of those gallon plastic water containers for his drinking supply. Country-dwellers will often refuse chlorinated water.

If the diarrhoea is mild and of short duration, give a meal of arrow-root gruel, made by slaking one heaped tablespoonful of powdered arrowroot with a little cold water, then gradually pouring on boiling water, stirring vigorously until the mixture clears and is almost transparent. Add two teaspoonfuls of granulated sugar and two tablespoonfuls of evaporated or goats milk and feed when cool. In severe cases, two raw egg-whites whisked up with two tablespoonfuls caster sugar and a dessertspoonful of brandy are helpful. Discontinue all starch or roughage and feed light meals of cooked meat – veal or rabbit for preference. Any protracted attack of the malady indicates that there is something more than a temporary internal disturbance; and if it is accompanied by high temperature the Veterinary Surgeon should be summoned without delay.

Dicken Medal for Animals: This is the highest award which can be made to a dog, and is given only on rare occasions. One of the outstanding recipients was Crumstone Irma, belonging to the late Mrs M.B. Griffin, B.E.M. Irma, in conjunction with a half-sister, was instrumental in locating 233 human casualties in bomb-debris, 21 of whom were recovered alive. Both these dogs worked free; and only their close sympathy with their trainer made it possible for her to read the various signals when a casualty was scented.

Diet (*see also* FOOD): The German Shepherd is not a difficult dog to feed if one keeps a few simple facts in mind, and really 'simple' is the operative word.

Like all other breeds, if he is well exercised he will have a good appetite, providing his medical history is normal. Only good quality food with as few mixtures as possible should be given. Our breed tends to overheat easily, and rich foods, or those which contain heating properties are only to be given in small quantities in very cold weather, if at all.

The basic food is naturally meat, and this should be given either raw or lightly cooked with as much of the fibre and gristle as the dog will take and digest. Unbleached tripe should be fed raw or very lightly cooked, as it contains valuable minerals and roughage. Pork and veal or ewe-mutton are quite unsuited to the dog's digestion. Avoid tinned or processed meat, also deep-frozen products except in emergencies or for convenience when travelling: the tough fibre or meat is lost in the preparation, and as a result the dog's jaws and intestines will not get the work they require to keep them healthy. Even the anal glands are not pressed clean as nature intended by the bulky excreta. These tasty preparations are usually relished by dogs; and they have their place in modern conditions, but only as auxiliary or occasional food — not for rearing puppies, nor for maintaining the hard, tough condition of this working breed and for creating firm muscles. For extra protein give egg-yolks — raw, of course — beaten in goats' milk wherever possible, or simply added to the main meal and well blended with the other ingredients.

A good quality *wholemeal* rusk or biscuit meal is advised, bought in the smallest quantities convenient to avoid dusty or stale-tasting meal. Best of all is wholemeal bread (*see* BISCUITS). Always store in dry airtight containers, as wholemeal does not keep well and easily becomes weevilly. We use small-sized new dustbins as the strongest and most convenient storage bins. Being round they can be moved more easily without lifting; and they are quite reasonably priced in comparison with the more refined article.

Finely grated raw carrots are a valuable addition (*see* CALCIUM DEFICIENCY). If overheating is noticed, also at times of changing the coat or for the purpose of hastening the 'bloom', give one tablespoonful of finely chopped watercress and parsley, added to and mixed with the main meal. Olive oil, being a true 'sunshine food', is most helpful in puppy rearing and for maintaining a healthy intestine and good coat in adult dogs. If it is bought in bulk form, that is gallon or half-gallon tins from health-food stores, it is cheaper than the small fancy bottles at the chemist or grocer. Start the small puppies on a few drops, and work up to a dessertspoonful daily for the adult in normal health. We would add a warning that 'salad' oils are unsuitable, as they are mostly produced from peanuts (arachide) or turnips (rape oil).

For weaning puppies, nursing bitches and elderly or sick dogs our faith has long been pinned on best quality semolina, medium ground. This also can be bought in bulk at a very reasonable cost (for the preparation *see* SEMOLINA).

Barley flakes (or kernels) are another excellent form of cereal food; and these do not require cooking—only soaking in hot water.

They are very soothing for any kind of kidney disorders. Oatmeal or flakes are too heating for the breed generally, and are not recommended.

Honey is a wonderful and indispensable food with a wide number of uses. It should not be cooked, as this destroys many of its best properties: melt it in warm water or milk, and most dogs will take it greedily. (*See* HONEY for full explanation of its uses.)

The best milk is from goats; but unless one keeps a nanny oneself this is not easy to obtain. Evaporated milk, which is constant in quality, is the next best choice, unless you have a cow; since bottled milk is seldom fresh and can cause 'scouring' in puppies. Tinned milk, like tinned meat, is of course convenient for travelling.

Broth made from fresh marrow-bones and/or sheep's or beast's heads with carrots, leeks, onions and plenty of garlic is splendid for condition and digestion, and helps to balance a diet which could be deficient in vitamins and mineral salts. Boil the bones or heads for an hour, then add the vegetables and cook another half-hour, strain, cool and keep in the refrigerator, heating quantities as required. It does not keep more than a few days even under refrigeration. Heat the quantity required to soak the rusk and stir up well – only sufficient to make a crumbly consistency is necessary: too soft foods are bad for both teeth and digestion.

Dry Coat: Check that the dog is in normal health with his usual appetite –abnormally cold or hot weather with high winds can dry a coat on an outside or working dog, and so can swimming, particularly in sea water. In any of these cases, shampoo the dog with a coconut oil shampoo and give a tablespoonful of olive oil daily. Also, use the hands to massage and stimulate the coat in the daily grooming, and finish with a soft wash-leather. A tablespoonful of finely grated suet is sometimes helpful, particularly if the meat ration is all lean or is tinned meat, which is usually fat-free. But give fresh butcher's suet, and mix it well in with the main meal so that it digests more easily.

Dryness of coat can indicate kidney trouble; if none of the above hints brings improvement, obtain professional advice.

Dry Elbows (*see* GROOMING).

Eagle, Look of: This expression is much used in America to express nobility, and sometimes creeps into our own reports.

Ears (*see also* CLEANLINESS and DEAFNESS): Puppies are born with the ears close to the head; and as the teeth develop they begin to move forwards sometimes in the form of a little cap. Usually by the fourth month they are fully erect. Puppies vary, however, considerably in the time taken to put up their ears; even within the same litter there are differences. One should not give up hope until about the end of the

first year, as a dog which is late with his permanent teeth may well be late also with his ear erection — as in human infants, ears and teeth have a great connection.

Some ear leathers are over-heavy and these, along with the paper-thin ones, seem to be the most uncertain in their elevation. When one looks at the pictures of the strange variety of ear carriage in the dogs which went to make our breed in the early days, it is easy to see how far we have come by our breeding efforts to creating a standard ear carriage. In actual fact, soft ears are encountered with lessening frequency.

Always warn anyone who caresses a puppy not to play with its ear-flaps, soft and tempting as they are. The tiny muscles are very delicate, and even rough play with litter-brethren can injure them. Care should also be exercised when putting puppies into a kennel that the ears are not knocked or damaged on the doors.

Ear carriage is only part of the head in the Standard; but it is one of the most easily noted faults if not correct. We are told that the ears should be moderately pointed, and carried open towards the front. The actual placement of the ears is as important as the carriage to the general appearance. Size, too, enters into the matter: over large or heavy ears detract from the noble expression, while undersize or sharply pointed ones give an untypical expression of a foxy or terrier-like kind. Fringes of hair are also faulty on the ears and spoil the expression. The hairs on the ears should be short and velvety in texture.

Ears, Soft (Remedy and Assistance): Although ear carriage does not figure largely in the Standard of points, it does affect the general appearance to a remarkable degree, and therefore assumes considerable importance. Should the ears not attain their proper erect position by 5-6 months, some assistance may be given, which often results in fixing a permanent position.

Begin by sketching the outline of the puppy's ear on a piece of paper. Copy this on a square of Chiropodist's Felt (obtainable from the chemist) and cut out the cone-shaped piece with sharp scissors

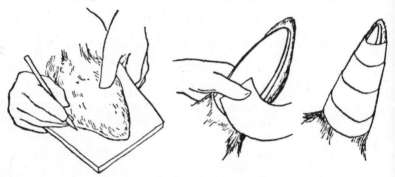

Correcting soft ear carriage by taping

(*see* illustrations). Snip the hair on the inside of the ear to avoid painful pulling, and coat with a layer of 'New Skin'. Then, while this is still 'tacky', insert the felt (adhesive side next to the 'New Skin') and hold for a few minutes until it feels firm. Next, take a self-adhesive bandage such as Prestoband and wind it in overlapping turns round the ear, starting from the base and taking care not to bend the ear in an unnatural position meanwhile. Secure the end well inside the last fold and leave for several days, renewing if necessary.

Some breeders maintain that weakness can be corrected by tying-up the puppy in the garden and calling him from an upstairs window! In all events, anything is worth trying in an attempt to remedy this fault.

Eczema: Most kinds of simple dermatitis can be checked and cured if taken from the onset. Small patches of red and irritated skin from which the fur has been either nibbled or scratched occur from time to time even on the healthiest dogs.

We bathe with a solution 50/50 of T.C.P. and warm water. Allow to dry, and coat with calamine lotion immediately, preventing the dogs from licking it as it sometimes makes them sick. If this is done twice daily for a few days it will usually clear up mild outbreaks. Many serious cases of eczema and its kindred diseases stem from neglect, so never leave a dog untreated — it can mean weeks of trouble ahead and considerable trouble, expense and suffering, not to mention the inconvenience of many dressings,

It is as well to give a course of condition powders when the skin eruptions appear, and to give 2-3 tablespoonfuls of finely chopped watercress and parsley on the main meal. Your veterinary surgeon will prescribe if the outbreak is widespread or prolonged; but quick action will often save having to call him.

Eggs: These are useful additions to the diet for extra protein and as a stimulant, if only yolks are used, raw for preference; and most dogs enjoy them. The strong albumen in the whites of eggs is not digested by a dog, and is useless and possibly harmful, particularly in young puppies and in adults which are used for breeding.

Excreta: Since the dog (even a German Shepherd!) cannot describe its symptoms in illness or warn us that it feels unwell, we must watch his eliminations daily to judge his state of health — many dogs owe their lives to the watchful eye of those in charge of their welfare through this medium.

Light-coloured motions usually indicate that the liver is not functioning properly: it is sometimes only necessary to exclude all fat and fatty substances from the diet for a few days to rectify this condition, giving a couple of condition powders each morning on a fasting stomach. Watch closely, however, for any signs of jaundice — the eyes give the first indication of the yellow colour symptomatic of this dread disease (*see* JAUNDICE).

A black motion of very hard consistency is also indicative of trouble —sometimes internal bleeding darkens the faeces. Without flying into a small panic, it is as well to keep a sharp eye on these functions; and if the signs of disorder are obvious, or if even slight ones are prolonged, then seek professional advice immediately.

Bones can cause light, crumbly motions. Always examine for any trace of bleeding and give light foods of soft consistency until healing is effected if this is not severe, when treatment is indicated.

The normal bowel action should be achieved without undue straining and the elimination a medium brown colour and well formed.

Elbows: The elbow plays a greater part in the front movement than is usually realised. Unless the joint is firm, with enough suppleness to take the shock of the free swinging to and fro of the front legs and also sudden changes of direction, it can spoil the clear sequence of steps and the harmony of the gait. A well-placed elbow is therefore of great importance in a good front assembly — one which is 'tied' in elbow is as weak in front as one with wide elbows. Neither supports the heavy front part of the body correctly or allows a proper flow of action. Both faults usually stem from a dietary deficiency causing weak bone, and are among the most difficult faults to eradicate. Breeders should be on their guard against perpetuating lines which carry this defect.

The skin on the elbows often becomes dry and scabby from the heavy dog lying on bare floors or earth. A daily touch with a mixture of 50/50 coconut fat and vaseline (*see* GROOMING) will counteract this. If the dog licks it, run an old nylon stocking into place over the joint and stitch it firmly to give the sore place a chance to recover: the stocking will be elastic enough to give freedom of movement. If the elbow is very sore, a light bandage should be fixed before rolling on the stocking, which should be of the 'stretch' variety.

English Dog Breeders: Dog fanciers in the British Isles are renowned the world over for the fine condition of their dogs; and if the Germans do not always approve of the structure or character of the Shepherds we produce, they are nonetheless full of admiration for the way our dogs are presented.

The chief difference between Continental and British breeders of Shepherds would appear to be that here there are large kennels housing numbers of Shepherds, while in their country of origin and in most European countries three to five dogs is more usual; and for this reason the disposition of their dogs is superior to ours since they receive more individual attention and live, as they were intended and originally bred to, close to man as his stalwart companion and guard with the chance to exercise their fantastic intelligence and capabilities.

Exercise: The German Shepherd requires plenty of exercise, but most of all he requires freedom. A large pen or enclosure, properly wired in chain link, where he can romp, jump and roll is essential if he is not a working dog: he will do all these things in the course of his day's work. The beautiful outline of a well-constructed Shepherd

needs firm muscles and ligaments, and these can be kept in condition
only by regular use. Stick retrieving and ball chasing—a large ball,
please!—can help his feet, pasterns and metatarsus. Swimming will
develop his shoulders and forechest: but take care that he is well
dried off with a large wash-leather and that his ears are examined
carefully afterwards. As these are wide open, water can enter and
cause distress, so swab them out gently with a soft piece of linen. But
first of all, give him ample chance to shake himself on coming out
of the water. This will free him of more water in a minute than you
can mop off him in an hour.

Road exercise, always on the lead, should be a daily occurrence
from six months onwards. This accustoms the dog to traffic noises
and people, teaches him a certain amount of discipline and wears
down his feet (and yours!). All dogs love their walks: the cries of
delight when the leads are brought out indicate how much they enjoy
their outings; and if afterwards they are dried and put to rest in a
draught-free kennel (not heated) they do not suffer, even in weather
when one would much rather remain indoors oneself. Alas! we have
chosen an active, demanding breed; and no amount of summer activity
can compensate for a winter spent by the fireside. Some exercise
should be given *every* day, or the dog will suffer, mentally as well as
physically. Let him sniff and attend to his wants for a while: but
unless he lives in country unfrequented by other dogs this sniffing
can constitute a danger. So restrict it as far as possible in towns and
public parks where disease abounds.

Hill climbing is excellent for shoulder development and the muscles
of the back. So if you live near a quarry or some safe cliff, encourage
him to climb and descend these whenever possible.

Exporting Dogs: In common with other breeds, German Shepherd Dogs
are exported to many countries overseas, many obtaining high honours
in the show world in their new homes. Prices asked are rather higher
than those for the home market, as the breeders must lose the dog
completely with no further chance of obtaining a puppy or using a
stud dog, and no reflected glory from a home show career. Only top
class specimens should ever be exported for the show ring; and if
puppies are sent, these should be really strong and healthy and of firm
character. Nobody has yet been able to guarantee that a puppy will
maintain his early promise, whether sold at home or overseas; but if
it is healthy and of reliable bloodlines it should prove a useful addition
to the new owner's stock, even if it does not become a Champion.

Export orders are best handed over to a reliable shipper for despatch: there are several who specialise in this work, and they are conversant with the size and type of kennel required, the best and fastest air and sea delivery services and will accompany the dog to airport or ship at hours highly inconvenient to ourselves. They also have personal contact with freight people and carriers, which ensures that their charges get the best attention, and their prices are most reasonable for the services given.

The Kennel Club issue Export Pedigrees on request, and will inform the vendor of any special restrictions existing in the country to which the dog is being exported. The cost of an Export Pedigree is £17.50.

Certificates must also be obtained from a Veterinary Surgeon to show that a male specimen is entire — this has to be presented to the Kennel Club before the Export Pedigree can be issued. Also, not more than 48 hours before the departure, a clean bill of health certificate is needed from the Veterinary Surgeon.

Export orders require much time and care, and all these extra items must be taken into account when quoting prices.

Expression: The expression comes from the eyes, which in a true Shepherd, good and typical, are a deep soft brown full of wisdom with an alert yet confident look, not showing fear. But there is expression,

Typical head and ear carriage

too, in the way the head is held, proudly and gracefully; and in the shape of the muzzle, neither Roman-nosed nor snipey, with tight lips and a well-pigmented nose. All this beauty speaks for itself, mirroring the incorruptibility, the closeness to mankind, the burning desire to please and vigilance for his owner's welfare which spell German Shepherd Dog to those of us who so dearly love our breed, and which attract new people into our ranks in ever increasing numbers.

Eyes (*see also* EXPRESSION): To the writer these are the true mirror of the dog's character and disposition. Almost almond shaped, set slightly obliquely and not in the least full, they should be a deep, soft brown, although a lighter shade is acceptable in a dog with a light muzzle.

Feet (*see also* CAT-FEET and CLAWS): These are a very important point in a working breed, and only correct keeping and much exercise can develop and maintain the well-muscled digits and tough pads required.

Puppies should be put on to concrete and rough ground as soon as weather and their health allows. Some are ready to creep about outside at 4 weeks in good weather. Let them do this, even for short periods, so that their first steps are in the right direction. Hill climbing and free running over uneven surfaces are excellent for both feet and shoulders; and all dogs should start their road exercise by 6 months old.

Fighting: The best cure is naturally prevention. Some dogs just cannot agree; and these cases must be kept separately, as besides the risk of battle they get worked-up and nervous, which can affect others in the kennel.

In the disagreeable event of an encounter, these are a few tips which may help to separate the combatants. A soda siphon squirted in the face will make them loosen their hold (if one should be handy), but take care to be ready to get one of them outside before they can come to grips again. A piece of cloth soaked in ammonia and held to the nostrils will also loosen the grip, by causing the dog to gasp for breath. Sometimes a sharp blow behind the ears with the edge of the hand will make the dog shake his head and loosen his hold on the victim. Never use pepper – it can cause terrible pain or even blindness, and is extremely cruel.

Fish: This is a useful item on the menu and most dogs enjoy it as a change. In sickness it is valuable, too, being easily digested and containing minerals to aid recovery.

Herrings are excellent. They should be beheaded and thrown into a large pan of water and brought to the boil for five minutes. Then drain and the backbone and sharp pieces of fin can be easily removed. The fine bones will not upset large breeds in normal health. Rock fish or cod fillet are good, but must be carefully boned by hand. Give roughly ½ lb. more fish than meat per dog, and add an egg yolk to the meal to balance. Sardines are wonderful for tempting convalescent dogs to eat, and, fed with the oil, very good for hurrying on the bloom after coating. Half a tin added to the normal meal 2 or 3 times a week will be enough.

Fleas: These pests are still very much with us, despite the modern anti-dotes. The only way to keep these disease-carriers at bay is to go through the dog's coat by back combing with a large comb at the most usual breeding-places — the root of the tail, along the spine, round the ears and chin, and between the digits, not forgetting the dew pads. With frequent inspection the pests will not develop to any extent if the coat is well powdered with any of the many reliable products sold for the purpose. There are medicated washes for heavy infestation; these are best obtained via your veterinary surgeon. Shield the dog's eyes and nostrils during either treatment, as the ingredients are highly irritant to these tender spots.

Food Bowls: Galvanised or aluminium ware is best for feeding bowls — enamel can chip, and the particles cause serious internal disorders, particularly in puppies, while earthenware will almost certainly be broken, and may occasion cuts or wounds through the dogs licking the fragments. Use a large bowl so that the food is less easily spilled over on to floors where there may be dust or germs; and always scour with boiling water after use. Never leave dirty feeding-bowls unwashed to attract flies which carry disease and perhaps disaster for your dog's health.

Food Preparation and Keeping: If there is one necessity where several dogs are kennelled, or where meat has to be bought in bulk quantities, it is a reliable refrigerator. Chilled meat, of course, should not be fed straight from refrigeration, but left in a warm room for at least an hour before feeding, taking out only as much as is required for each meal.

If the dogs' meals are prepared on a table, it is a good idea to provide some protection for the food bowls during preparation, in case one is called away before all is ready. We have found a few yards of butter-muslin the best covering; it can be suspended from a coat-hanger hung from a hook in the ceiling and thus easily swung to one side when not in use. This makes a kind of tent over the food and bowls, at low cost, and is more effective and easier to remove than individual covers. Fly-blown food is a great source of danger, particularly to small puppies.

Rusk and biscuit must be stored in damp- and vermin-proof containers — large biscuit tins are useful for small quantities; or the smaller sized galvanised refuse bins are excellent, reasonably priced and long lasting for bulk buying in larger establishments. A few pounds wisely spent on strong, good quality equipment can save much waste, and perhaps even sickness and loss of precious time.

A couple of saucepans in either aluminium or stainless steel are essential for making large or small quantities of broth or porridge for puppies — enamel may chip and is thus dangerous as well as short-lived in hard daily use. An outsize galvanised boiler for cooking meat, etc., is also necessary. We do not advocate a pressure cooker, as the high temperature destroys the protein and fibre in the meat, making it pappy and not suitable to a dog's digestion which functions best on coarse fibre and plenty of roughage.

If the olive oil used is kept in a bottle with a plastic pourer top it saves time, waste and patience.

A vegetable shredder of the type used in the Swiss 'Bircher-Benner' Health Clinic is available at most health-food stores, and is ideal for carrots, etc.

Food Quantities: This is one of the most frequently posed questions; and the answer is endless, as the amount of food varies greatly according to the age, the amount of exercise given, etc. Moreover dogs, like people, seem to have different rates of metabolism, some using up and therefore requiring larger amounts of food than others.

Some lines have a tendency to 'run to fat'. So it is as well to have a look at the dog's relations, to see whether he is heavily or lightly built: then restrict or increase the amounts accordingly. Also check up that some kind or misguided person in your household is not supplementing the dog's diet with tit-bits, ruining its appetite and digestion and making it dainty about its correct nourishment.

Generally 1–1½ lb. of good meat for bitches, and 1½–2 lb. for dogs is the daily requirement of an animal in normal health. If more is given, the rusk, etc., is not eaten; and although meat is a dog's natural food and his first requirement, he has become domesticated and some wholewheat cereal is also an essential part of his diet, since he is deprived of much of the gristle and tough skin of freshly-killed meat. For dogs kept indoors, too, an all meat diet can make them smell strongly. So make about one-third of the bulk food good quality wholemeal rusk or biscuit.

Half a pint of milk — goat's for preference — is a good addition. It contains natural calcium and is a useful vehicle for condition powders, etc.

One large teaspoonful of olive oil daily on the food also helps intestinal functions and gives a gleam to the coat. Double the amount for a dog lacking condition.

One tablespoonful of finely grated carrot, and one of well-chopped parsley or watercress is excellent for the blood stream. Two or three tablespoonfuls of 'health broth' (see DIET) to soak the biscuit or rusk is sufficient.

Quantities for growing puppies and litters are indicated under the appropriate headings.

Food Refusal: This is usually associated with the exercise of that name in the obedience test in the Open class; and very useful it would be if all dogs could be taught to refuse food offered by strangers, as many good dogs have been lost by poisoning through the medium of the deadly dose disguised in some tasty tit-bit.

A dog which refuses food at his usual feeding time is usually in some way a sick dog. If he appears listless or poorly, take his temperature, and call the Veterinary Surgeon if it is more than 102° or less than 100° — the normal being 101.5° Fahrenheit.

If the dog appears hungry but will not eat, lift up the bowl and try him again later. He may have some discomfort after eating grass or have become excited from romping, and not feel in the mood to eat. Take a look at the meat, too, to see that all is well: some frozen kinds are put in a state of preservation when deterioration has already begun; and this can be as revolting to the dog as it is to ourselves.

Some dogs refuse to eat in a strange place, or even a different-from-usual place in their own kennels. Here a little patience and coaxing is all that is needed.

Don't worry unduly if a dog misses just one meal — most of them are the better for an occasional fast, provided it is not for more than 24 hours and no symptoms of illness are manifested.

Foster Mothers: Large litters are more the rule than the exception in Shepherd Dogs, but six, or eight at the most, is the largest number of puppies which can properly and conveniently be reared by the dam. So it is sometimes expedient to obtain a foster-mother for the 'surplus' puppies if they are normal in health and worth saving: sometimes, by reason of some especially interesting blood lines or because there is a big demand for a puppy from that particular litter, it is decided to rear all of them.

Of course, if through whelping complications (fortunately rare in this breed) a foster becomes necessary, a glance through any of the weekly dog papers will give you the address of a reliable source. When the foster-bitch arrives, take her a little run on the lead so that she is comfortable, and mark the spot where she urinates: as soon as possible afterwards rub your own puppies with the results, or squeeze some of her milk gently on to a clean piece of cloth and rub it on the young ones. This will give her the impression she is nursing her own babies quicker than anything, as they will carry her scent. Keep a sharp watch on her for the first 24 hours: these fosters are usually experienced and offer no objection to caring for their adopted babies; but if they are off colour or upset, they can be troublesome and need supervision until they settle down. Keep your own bitch as far away as possible, of course, or you may have a jealous battle on your hands.

Gait (*see* ACTION).
Garlic: This best of the 'lilies of the field' is a great friend of the dog. There is a small press which can be bought for a few pence which squeezes the juice out; and if a teaspoonful is added to the dog's main meal it will help condition or recovery from illness, increase the appetite and generally tone up the system. For puppies half this quantity will greatly decrease the activity of round worms and help digestion. It is one of the finest purifiers of the blood. Add it to their broth, or buy it in capsule form if more convenient.
German Shepherd Dog League (*see* ALSATIAN LEAGUE).
Gestation, Period of: The normal period is 63 days as for other breeds; but a bitch can go down with her litter quite safely after 58-59 days, so that one should be prepared and not rely on her lasting the full period. Do not, however, allow her to exceed the given time: a dead or malformed puppy may be the cause of the delay. So summon veterinary attention and keep the mother under constant supervision if the arrival of the first puppy is unduly delayed.

During these 63 days, the bitch will have followed more or less her usual routine – the more normal the better, her daily exercise, without any jumping, being an all important factor. A 3-grain tablet of the herb Raspberry Leaf night and morning is most beneficial, toning up the muscles and keeping the bloodstream pure for the great day of the puppies' arrival. The appetite may be erratic at these times, particularly in the early and late weeks; but coax the mother-to-be with the kind of food she prefers (even if it is something she would not dream of eating when in her usual condition!). Keep her intestine working normally by small regular doses (1 dessert spoon) of ½ liquid paraffin and ½ olive oil.

Establish her whelping-quarters and see that she sleeps there, after being gradually introduced, for the last two weeks. It is a good plan to sacrifice an evening or two to this. Take a comfortable chair − a deck chair is fine − into her new quarters, wrap yourself in a rug if cold, and read a book or paper for half an hour: she will soon grasp the idea that all is well and settle down to rest and make her nest. She should be exercised as late and as early as possible; bitches cannot wait comfortably at these periods, and much damage can be caused by failing to give this point due thought.

Good, lean meat, not cut too fine, is her best form of food at these times, with plenty of honey given in full cream fresh dairy milk or evaporated milk diluted 50/50. An egg yolk and a dessertspoonful of olive oil of the best quality, added to the daily meal, will give her the extra vitamins she requires. Feed her the grated carrot as suggested, also chopped parsley and watercress − a mixed tablespoonful each day. Any cereal feed now should be wholemeal and in limited quantities as a 'fat one' can have trouble delivering her litter. Plan everything well ahead and your expectant mother will be confident and relaxed when the great moment comes.

Glamour: Used sometimes to describe an attractive or striking dog, and really far from suitable as a word to fit a hard-conditioned working dog as our breed should be. It is better left for film stars.

Goat's Milk: It is a pity this is so hard to come by commercially. Most dogs love it, and it is of the greatest help in sickness or convalescence. With a large dessertspoonful of honey and a little warm water added it will revive your dog after a long day outside in the wet; and a dog can be perfectly safe on a fast for 24 hours on 2 or 3 of these drinks.

Gravy (*see also* BROTH): 'Made-up' or thickened gravies should not be given: they overheat the blood and are too rich for the digestion. Beef tea, made by pouring warm water on gravy beef and leaving over-night, is good for stimulating a sick dog which is in a low state from lack of food. Weak Marmite is also good, but not meat essences which are highly seasoned and contain preservatives.

Grooming: This is an art, even in a comparatively short-coated breed such as the G.S.D. First of all, see that you (or those whose task it is to groom your dogs) have the proper equipment.

A handy box-cum-tray, of the sort used for boot brushes, is ideal for keeping the necessary items together and convenient for use, if small compartments are made as in the illustration overleaf.

Start by standing your dog on a sturdy table. He will quickly learn to jump up; and this has an additional use, as when he enters a Show and has to be 'vetted' he will get on the table without hesitation, anticipating the pleasure of his daily grooming. This is no small help when trying to enter a show with several dogs and their 'luggage' not to mention those of several other breeds milling around one's feet.

Now look in your dog's mouth, ears and eyes for any sign of trouble. (A broken tooth or an abscess in embryo is not easily seen without close examination.) Take a glance at his pads, and under his tail to see if any sign of tapeworm segments are there. During this looking-over the presence of any vermin can be detected: and the immediate application of some D.D.T. or Gammexane powder of one of the reputable makes will usually bring matters under control and, perhaps, check an outbreak in the kennel.

Run a comb backwards through the dog's coat. Any sign of infestation, hedge tears or cuts, skin eruptions, etc., can then be spotted and remedied with the handy contents of the 'beauty box': many a large bill for treatment could be avoided by simple remedies applied at the right time – the onset of trouble.

Then brush the coat in a rotary motion to cleanse it, and finally 'set' it back by lightly combing the right way and brushing deeply to bring out the gleam. Finish with a final polish with a soft wash-leather and apply a small quantity of 'elbow grease' on the elbow joints – also hock bones if necessary – massaging gently into the skin. The whole operation takes 10–15 minutes, but is worth every second: the dogs enjoy it, it gets young ones accustomed to intimate handling and makes them feel important while receiving attention. Every Shepherd yearns to be a 'one and only' at heart, even if he enjoys canine companionship occasionally.

Here are the items required for the seven compartments: two brushes, one of stiff whalebone, the other softer for the underbelly and flanks; a strong comb, not too fine or it will break the outer coat; a piece of chamois leather; a hound glove; a packet of cleansing tissues; a 'squeezie' plastic bottle of T.C.P.; a tin of insect powder; a tin with a hole in the lid to take ribbon-type cotton wool (sometimes these jobs have to be done single-handed, so it is best to choose containers which dispense their contents easily); strong nail clippers for a broken claw and a pair of square-ended forceps have their obvious uses. A 'squeezie' plastic bottle of boracic lotion (medium strength) and one of the Cortisone eye ointments may also be included.

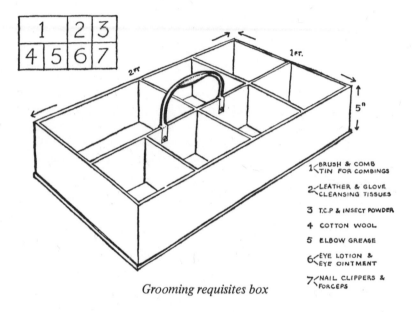

Grooming requisites box

1 < BRUSH & COMB
     < TIN FOR COMBINGS

2 < LEATHER & GLOVE
     < CLEANSING TISSUES

3 T.C.P & INSECT POWDER

4 COTTON WOOL

5 ELBOW GREASE

6 < EYE LOTION &
     < EYE OINTMENT

7 < NAIL CLIPPERS &
     < FORCEPS

The 'elbow grease' housed in a plastic pot (glass is one of a dog owner's pet aversions) is used daily in our kennel, and is made by melting equal quantities of white vaseline and coconut fat — we buy ¼ lb. of each — in an old tin over a low heat. Stir it well and pour into your pot when cool. (Keep it away from the greedy, who will eat it and make themselves sick!) If a small supply is rubbed into the dry skin on the elbows it will keep them supple and prevent cracks and soreness; and if used constantly from youth will in most cases maintain the growth of hair on this vulnerable spot. Dogs which lie on carpets are the worst sufferers of this blemish, which can be painful if neglected.

Add to your equipment a tin to stuff the combings into for tidiness' sake, and you are equipped to deal with many small emergencies without wasting time running to the medicine chest, and also with

the wherewithal to give each dog the hallmark of proper care and attention – neat feet, clean eyes and ears, and a gleaming, odour-free coat.

Growth: A German Shepherd makes all his major growth in his first
year: afterwards he develops and matures. Much patience is needed,
particularly by novice owners, as a fine puppy can suddenly become a
gangling yearling – especially a dog – and it takes from 3–6 months
to recover its balance and form. Meanwhile, it is usually best to give
him a rest from the show ring and concentrate on body-building foods;
egg yolks, semolina porridge and honey, and our priceless friend garlic.
Our breed frequently goes on improving up to three or four years old,
and lasts on for years in youthful health and condition. So it is easily
understood that they are not to be hurried in their early development.

Guide Dogs for the Blind: No work on the German Shepherd would be
complete without a reference to this best of all the many tasks to
which their unusual intelligence fits them so completely.

This voluntary movement was founded in the late 1920s by Mrs
Eustis, an American lady who during a visit to Germany saw the dogs
which were trained to guide and assist those blinded in the Great War.
She received a decoration for her great work in America. In Great
Britain, the Committee for the movement has always included several
of our well-known breeders and judges, notably the late Lady Shuster,
Lady Kitty Ritson and, perhaps best known of all, the late Miss Muriel
Crooke, R.A., who devoted a great part of her life, always modestly
avoiding the limelight, to this splendid cause.

Handlers: These are persons, usually paid or professional, who will take
a dog for training and presenting in the show ring. Before the war
they were practically non-existent in this breed, being mostly associated
with the terrier and gun-dog breeds. Now that the day of the big
establishment is virtually at an end and kennel-staff are difficult to
find as well as highly paid in comparison to former times, it is becoming
an economic necessity to employ a handler if several entries are made
by one staff-less owner at the same show. Three to four pounds for
each class is the average fee charged, with handsome bonuses in addition
for wins in Open classes or for Challenge Certificates.

A dog with the deep devotion to its owner common to this breed
will often show better and appear more alert in strange hands; and if
friendly help is not forthcoming, one of the several handlers should be
approached – in plenty of time as they are usually booked heavily for
the show season.

In America this is a recognised profession having its own union. The members are highly qualified and usually shrewd judges of a dog, who will not accept the task of presenting it unless it is a potential top winner, so that their influence is considerable in the show ring.

Hardpad: This is a virus disease like distemper, and has many of the same symptoms. The pads of the feet become hard and shiny during the illness, which carries a high mortality-rate and is dreaded by all breeders.

Vomiting, diarrhoea and a soaring temperature are noticed, and these may appear to have been brought under control only for fits to occur after a variable period, showing that encephalitis (inflammation of the brain) has developed. In this case it is best for all concerned to help the poor sufferer to a painless end.

Heads: More than anything, the head of a G.S.D. personifies the breed: the nobility of a well-bred specimen is so perfectly displayed in the clean-cut, aristocratic profile, the broad skull without coarseness

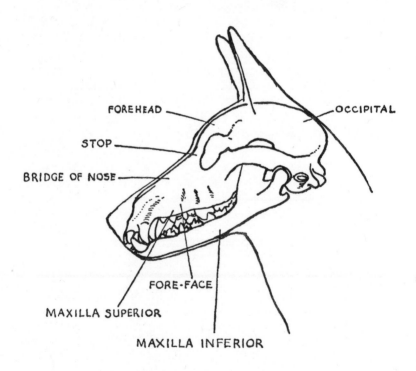

Details of head construction

but with plenty of room for brains, the tight line of the lips free from 'slobbering', and the deep brown of the almond-shaped eye with its lovely expression of quiet vigilance, ready to take care of any danger that might threaten the beloved owner.

In the head, too, is expressed what we call sex quality; and here the dog should have a bolder, bigger head with larger ears and a rather jaunty, masculine way of looking around him peculiar to his sex; while the bitch is more refined of features with a quieter, more intense expression in her eyes which rarely leave her owner. In judging the breed, we lay stress on sex-characteristics, many of which are shown in the head.

Hearing (*see* EARS).

Heat (or Oestrum): The oestral period or 'season' lasts for an average of three weeks and is heralded by frequent inclination to urinate and swelling of the vulva followed by a coloured discharge. This lasts for from 10–15 days in our breed; and on an average the bitch is usually ready for mating about the 14th day, although we have had them refuse a dog's attentions until as late as the 21st day. Bitches are sometimes very individual in this respect; and only from actual experience can the right day be discovered, when it should be noted for future reference.

An increase in appetite is sometimes a sign of approaching 'jolly times' – as they were called in the old books on dogs; and if you do not wish your bitch to be 'jolly', there are several useful modern products to help you keep her intact, besides the obvious one of keeping her in an enclosure proof against egress as well as ingress. We give two veterinary Amplex tablets three times daily for the first week, three thrice daily from 7–12 days, and three four times daily from 12–18 days, reverting to two thrice daily for one week more. The first dose is given *before* the morning exercise and the last on shutting up at night. One of the several Aerosol sprays is most helpful if squirted on the 'pants', and also along the bottom of kennel doors and run gates where unwanted suitors may sniff. However, all these products must be discontinued at least three days before mating is to be attempted, or the weapon may recoil and the stud dog decide that the lady is not interesting.

Bitches are often extra affectionate and sensitive at these times, and inclined to resent others of their sex. So it is as well to keep an eye on them, if several run together, in order to preserve good personal relationships.

Finally, when the 'colour' is no longer in evidence, wash the hind-quarters in Canex soap and warm water containing a little T.C.P. or Dettol, and leave several days clear before allowing her to run freely with the dogs again.

Hepatitis: Another 'killer' disease, with similar symptoms to distemper or even hardpad (but without the affection of the pads). It is highly contagious, and is spread and contracted via the urine, so restrict to a minimum your dog's enthusiasm for sniffing in parks and public places when exercising.

Herding Dogs (H.G.H. = Herdengebrauchshund): German Shepherd Dogs, as one might expect from their name, are often expert herding-dogs, although this ability is dying-out in some British strains from lack of use. They are still much used on the Continent by small and large farmers as herding and guard dogs combined – a dual role they are especially well equipped for filling. It is a familiar sight in some of the lonely districts of Europe to see a peasant with his motley flock of a couple of goats, a pony or donkey and some geese and hens all grazing along the side of a busy road under the eagle eye of a Shepherd Dog in perfect control of the situation.

One of the best herding strains comes from the blood of Grand Ch. Hettel Uckermark H.G.H. I remember the late Mrs M.B. Griffin, B.E.M., had a bitch she called Echo which worked both sheep and cattle on her farm in New Zealand, and which came down from Hettel.

In this country we already have a number of indigenous breeds which herd, and one does not see many German Shepherds at this task. However, their natural ability is becoming recognised and the numbers are increasing, which is pleasing to those who possess a herding strain.

Honey: There is no better friend of the dog-breeder than this wholesome and comparatively inexpensive commodity. Bought in large containers it costs about 60p per lb., and is invaluable for puppy rearing, sick dogs, or to combat a spell of bitterly cold weather such as the winters of 1962-63 and 1978-79. Honey must *not* be cooked or put into very hot liquid, as this destroys many of its great properties. For this reason, too, do not buy worthless 'blends' or honey that is not guaranteed as being extracted without heat.

A nervous, excited dog will calm down after a drink of warm milk and honey (a dessertspoonful melted in warm water with the un-heated milk added) with two calcium tablets crushed up and added. Honey and warm water with a little brandy added will revive an ex-hausted dog or help a heart-spasm. Honey for young puppies, too – a teaspoonful for each puppy in their two milk and porridge feeds each day. And honey for your old dogs, soothing and comforting to their digestions. Gingerbread made with honey is our dogs' birthday cakes! Harmless and wholesome, but it is difficult to keep them out of the kitchen when it's baking.

House-training: It is quite possible to house-train a puppy of three months or over in a week or two, if one is generous with time and patience.

Puppies, like babies, usually relieve themselves on awakening, so immediately your puppy has finished his nap put him outside, going with him the first few times, and wait until his duties are performed before returning to the house. Praise him at each performance in the right place, and you will be surprised how quickly he learns and even waits to go out. He cannot, at this age, last all night, and you must take him to your room and put his bed close to your own, so that you are aware of his movement. Put on a warm coat and take him outside – usually twice during the first two nights is necessary: then once for two or three nights until he sleeps from midnight to six a.m. and it is safe to leave him in the kitchen or some room with an uncarpeted floor. Do not keep him with you longer than is necessary, or he may cry and be restless when he is left alone again at night, and this will make him dirty.

He will need exercising when he has been fed, too. So be ready to put him out as soon as he leaves his feeding bowl. Don't stint him of water – a cruel trick often practised by unthinking owners – but 'no liquids after 9 p.m.' is a good rule.

If he is persistently dirty despite watchfulness, check him for worms which are often the cause of uncontrollable habits. A rolled-up newspaper, secured with an elastic band, to give him a light tap on the hindquarters, is a safe method of chastisement: the noise is more punishment than the tap to a sensitive breed such as ours. Use the voice with a firm note: never shout at a small puppy, nor chastise with the hand, which should only be associated with caresses or fondling.

In the event of a mistake on the carpet, quickly squirt the spot with a siphon if available. Then shampoo with 1001 or any other carpet cleaner immediately. A little ground coffee on a heated shovel wafted about the room removes odours quickly and pleasantly.

Hysteria: This distressing condition would seem to be on the wane in the last few years, due (largely) to the campaign against bleached flour in dog biscuit and meal. In the writer's opinion, too, smaller kennels make a contribution to the decrease: dogs are prone to imitation, and one restless and excitable animal will work up others, especially the young which are in the throes of glandular disturbance at the time of puberty, and bring on a fit or convulsion.

Cover the poor victim as quickly as possible in a heavy coat or blanket — light is his worst enemy at this moment. He may involuntarily snap and bite, as he is not aware of his actions at these times. Keep him in a cool, darkened place for some time, and give only water sweetened with honey to drink — no food for 24 hours is our cure — and a dessertspoonful of T.C.P. in a little warm water 3 times per diem for three or four days after the attack.

If the convulsions persist and are of an epileptic nature, call in your veterinary surgeon. Above all, remain calm yourself and don't imagine your dog will die in an attack. He may only be teething badly, or just growing up. So help him recover by a quiet, sensible approach and prompt removal to a darkened room.

Inbreeding: This, as the name suggests, is breeding a bitch back to a closely-related dog such as an uncle or cousin (*not* sire or brother which is termed incestuous breeding).

This can be a short cut to improving the strain; but largely speaking it is dangerous unless controlled by some very knowledgeable breeder with much experience of breeding down the particular line upon which the experiment is being made. Never lose sight of the fact that faults, as well as virtues, can be intensified by this method; and although in very experienced hands, and then often after expensive and disappointing trials, type can be established and strengthened, it is not a part of the average breeder's programme.

Insurance: The G.S.D. League and the B.A.G.S.D carry adequate insurance for their members. If you wish to insure for whelping risks or any special occasions there are several reliable brokers who place these risks. The premiums are fairly high, but may well be worth the expense if any real risk is involved.

Interdigital Cysts (and Eczema): These painful and annoying cysts appear quite frequently in otherwise healthy dogs; and some veterinary surgeons consider that they are a symptom of a skin ailment elsewhere in the dog. We use hot fomentations of T.C.P. and water. Blot them dry with cleansing tissues or old linen, and paint with Gentian Violet. Some dogs, however, will not respond to treatment and require a course of injections or even surgery if the cysts are large enough to cause lameness.

For eczema, we coat with Calamine lotion, dust thickly with boracic and zinc powder, and tie the bandaged foot up in an old nylon stocking to prevent licking.

Importing Dogs: Before going abroad to buy a German Shepherd Dog try if you can to visit two or three of the best known quarantine kennels: staff and managements change, and it is wise and prudent to see where the breed is especially favoured and will have the best attention.

If a bitch is imported 'in whelp' her puppies may be removed at weaning time, although she must remain in quarantine the full six months.

Visit the poor prisoner as frequently as possible, remembering that he or she has almost certainly left a loving home and must be confused and lonely in the restricted life of quarantine. If the dog has been trained − and most German ones have − give him a short period of work whenever possible: it will give him something to think about and he will be easier to handle when he emerges into his new world.

A little present to those in charge of the dog is acceptable; and you may find it is also permitted to take the dog some extras in the way of tasty or nourishing food, and a large bone to play with in the long hours of confinement.

It is better to import the dog in the early spring, so that he is not inactive in the restriction of quarantine during the cold months, when chills and rheumatism threaten even those who are well housed if they are deprived of long walks and ample freedom.

Quarantine and the various attendant expenses are costly and only really justified for a particularly fine specimen of the breed which can be widely used in the breeding programme in this country. Thus, great care and thought should be exercised in the choice of an import if it is to be worthwhile.

Intestines: As in all life, this is the seat of good health; and in these days of preserved and refined food it is *highly important* to supervise its functions. Ample food of a coarse and bulky nature is essential, especially in town dwelling dogs and those deprived of free exercise where the various grasses are chosen by the dog himself for medical purposes. Feed the meat in large chunks − at least 2-in. square for adults. Give proper wholemeal rusk or biscuit, olive oil, and parsley with watercress either dried or fresh. Plenty of fresh water, and all the exercise you can conveniently manage for him.

In the event of an obstruction or prolonged constipation, give an enema of two pints of water at blood heat with a large tablespoonful of olive oil added to the water, using a gravity douche and regulating a very gentle flow. This can be quite conveniently done by hanging the douche on a hook in the yard over or near a drain in readiness for the results of the washing-out. *See* CONSTIPATION for remedies for a lazy intestine; and to bring relief in severe cases massage the stomach and move the hind legs in a rotary or 'bicycling' action with the dog on his back.

In-Whelp Bitches (*see* PREGNANCY).

Irritation: If the dog scratches enthusiastically, you may be almost certain that fleas or lice are present, and must take the necessary action (*see* FLEAS). But if the scratching is laboured or aimed at one point, then examine for a skin eruption or swelling, and do not exclude bee-stings, indicated by a mottled swelling. After sponging the sting with cold, preferably iced water, pack bicarbonate of soda on it to form a cake. This will usually bring down the swelling and soothe the poor patient.

Isolation: When returning from shows, particularly if you have young stock or puppies, it is a wise precaution to disinfect the exhibits by swabbing mouths with T.C.P. on damp cottonwool, and to rub over the pads and 'pants' with a cloth dipped in a strong solution of disinfectant. Keep these dogs apart for 24 hours, in case any germ is incubating, and take temperatures if you are in doubt or have any suspicion of infection at the show. Sickness is expensive and time-wasting, and these simple precautions may save you a lot.

Ivory Bone: A descriptive term used sometimes in show critiques to describe the correct, rather flat clean bone required by our Standard, particularly on the front legs, where round bone is a fault.

Jackets: German Shepherds, being hardy outdoor animals, do not require 'coats', that is coats as worn by many other breeds in bad weather. The exception is the show dog in very wet weather and the sick dog.

For the former, one can save the back panel of a worn plastic mackintosh. Pierce a hole in each corner of a piece large enough to cover the dog's back with a V-shaped flap to fall over his croup. Pass two tapes under his body and fasten them through the holes, one tape just behind the forelegs and the other just forward of the hindlegs, and you can get your dog from car to bench without damaging his bloom. This jacket is not intended for wear when running free, only as an inexpensive aid to exhibitors in our unhelpful climate.

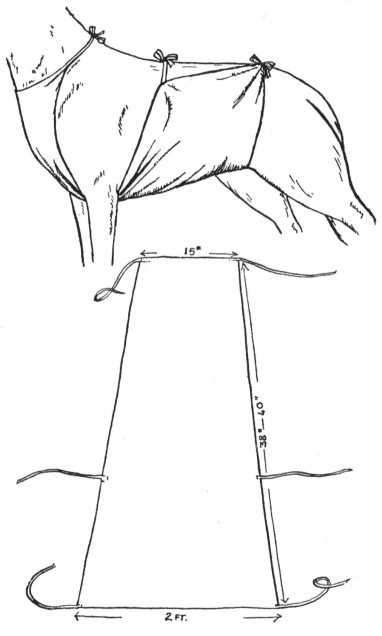

Pneumonia jacket

A jacket for a dog with a chill, or distemper, must fasten along the back and cover the chest. For this you need a piece of thin blanket or heavy woollen material, oblong in shape and long enough to cover the dog from chest to loins. Cut it rather narrower at the chest end, stitch the narrow end down with strong oversewing in a hem wide enough to take a strong tape, and draw a tape through it. This fastens collarwise round the dog's neck − it will be bunched up, and therefore loose and comfortable. Fasten two more tapes, stitched one each side, behind the shoulders, and two more above the loins. The aim is to cover the chest and brisket until the dog recovers. One advantage of this kind of home-made jacket is that small widths can be snipped from either end, so that the patient can be gradually 'returned to normal' with his extra covering diminishing in small doses.

Jaundice (Leptospirosis): A painful malady spread by rats; in humans it is sometimes called 'Miners' Disease'. It is caused by rats running over the food taken below by miners and passing urine thereon.

The 'whites' of the dog's eyes turn yellow, he refuses food, and there is usually a gastro-enteric haemorrhage which can easily and quickly prove fatal unless veterinary help is sought without delay. Give milk with a pinch of bicarbonate of soda while awaiting the Veterinary Surgeon and keep the dog on a fat-free diet for some weeks after he is cured. Prevention is largely in our hands, and rats should be exterminated by all known means, and dogs regularly inoculated.

Jelly: Make from lean gravy beef soaked in lukewarm water for a few hours: the liquid is then strained-off and set with some unflavoured gelatine dissolved in very hot water. The jelly can also be chilled, when it is often gratefully licked by a sick dog − it does not nauseate like some commercial preparations, and glucose can be incorporated when cool for added strength.

Jolly Times: In some old books on dogs this is the term for 'heat' or 'season', and one may still hear it among country folk in some districts. Actually it is rather a nice description, and we regret it is not more frequently used.

Judging: The task of judging a ringful of dogs, many of excellent quality, even the cream of the breed, is not one to be taken on lightly or because one would like the honour of the appointment. It is essentially an honour, and one which should be given only to breeders who have had useful and lengthy experience in the breed and also, naturally, are people of high integrity and not likely to use their engagements to further their own or their friends' kennels.

Our major breed clubs have judges' lists from which names can be selected, these people having been 'vetted' by the committees and given their support.

Entries are so large in our breed that one should get to bed in good time the night previous to one's engagement. If a lady, wear a skirt which allows one to bend to examine the dogs in comfort. A hat, when judging outdoors, is essential: in hot weather one can get a nasty burn standing in the sun absorbed in one's task, and in windy weather one is protected and at ease. When I was working up an attack of nerves over my first appointment, I asked the advice of one of our famous 'all-rounders'. His reply still amuses me: it was 'Give it to the B . . . you would like to take home with you and wear a comfortable pair of shoes.' . . . Very sound advice, really. Take a flask of hot coffee and something light to nibble, as one is always miles from the refreshment tent and mealtimes vary — I have had luncheon by 3 p.m.!

In our country, judging is by invitation after proposals to a show committee have been made by breeders or the breed member of that Society. In Germany it is a vastly different matter, and they have, comparatively speaking, very few judges. Each one has served a long apprenticeship beside a qualified Judge in his ring; and he must pass an examination and be approved by the 'S.V.' as the Verein Für Deutsche Schäferhunde is known. In this way type is preserved and character invariable in the winning dogs — indeed, one of the first impressions one gains on entering the famous Sieger-Show with its 800 dogs (normal entry) is that all the dogs look alike. In Canada, one is given a small show or match to judge as a trial, and one or two members of the Kennel Club for that area come along to watch one's performance. It is something worse than passing a driving test! If all goes well, one is given a judge's licence, and this is revoked for any kind of offence against their rules, or if persistently bad reports come in about one's judging. In the U.S.A., judges are licensed after trial, and it is a similar story. Considering how free and open our system is, we have very few cases of dishonest or incompetent judging.

One should always remember that prize cards are used as sales propaganda — Challenge Certificates even more so. So never give a major award to a specimen which is not worthy of being bred from, and whose type you do not consider should be perpetuated. Next year's puppies will be bred from this year's winners; and the judges are responsible in a very large measure for the future of the breed.

Jumping: All dogs like to jump: it is at once their manner of expressing pleasure and of attracting attention. However, a large breed such as ours can cause damage by leaping on visitors unprepared for their weight and exuberance. So discourage your puppies from jumping; and with older dogs push your knee into the chest as the dog springs forward, with the command firmly given 'Down!' This will hurt him without doing him harm, and he will soon learn his lesson.

Jumping, of course, is one of the exercises in dexterity in the Police Dog trials, when the dog must scale a wall of hard boards and leap ditches.

Junket: Prepared from unflavoured essence of rennet and sweetened with honey this is excellent for old dogs or convalescents from enteritis. It can with advantage be chilled for leptospirosis patients.

Keep, Cost of: Three pounds per week for food is a fair average of the cost of keeping an adult G.S.D. in normal health. Of course, if you buy luxury (and unnecessary) foods, or refined items more suited to toy breeds, you may easily double the expense and probably halve the dog's health. Puppies cost between £2 and £3 more per week, as they need quantities of milk and extra quality foods to give them a fair start.

Kennel Club: The Kennel Club is absolute ruler over dogdom, and if its rules are broken then fines are imposed or alternatively suspension from showing and judging for various periods. For serious offences, suspension can be even for life, which is virtually the end of the kennels owned by the offender, since it means that stud dogs owned by the person concerned cannot be used nor stock be registered from his or her kennels.

However, the Kennel Club is not all severity and does a great deal, much of it behind the scenes, to keep the sport on the right lines and to foster schemes for canine health research, and to encourage good fellowship with fine social events for those who are admitted to its rather limited membership. The Gun Dog Trials are, of course, one of the highlights of the sporting calendar and are well attended by famous 'shots' and people of note and rank.

Most breeders register all puppies with the Kennel Club; and when the puppies are sold the registration must be transferred to their new owners — forms are obtained from the Club. No dog can be entered at a show unless registered in the name of its present owner. Agreements for the loan of bitches on breeding terms can also be registered at the Kennel Club. In short, the Club is there to help and protect the dog breeder in all ways.

Rules can be obtained from Headquarters, so can registration and transfer forms; and the *Kennel Club Gazette*, issued monthly, is a mine of information on shows, new rules, transfers, new registrations, etc., and is really a *must* for all seriously engaged in dog breeding. The Chief Executive is Mr D. Adams, The Kennel Club, Clarges Street, Piccadilly, London W1Y 8AB.

Kennels, Cleaning of: This task must quite often be undertaken by the breeder, now that kennel staff are a dying race. These are a few of our own simple rules which, we like to think, make our dogs comfortable and pleasant to be near and keep them healthy.

For the greater part of the year, we give 2 or 3 clean sacks as bedding. These are removed once a week (accidents excepted), soaked in a weak Dettol solution, rinsed, and put through a mangle to facilitate drying. In very cold or damp weather, give a small amount of good quality woodwool, and change it as often as it is damp or soiled. When the dogs come in damp, put 2 or 3 large sheets of newspaper over the bedding to absorb the moisture and remove them last thing at night.

Wash out the kennels thoroughly once weekly — walls, doors, etc. — with warm suds made with carbolic soap, with your pet disinfectant added. Do *not* use detergents unless the kennels are rinsed with clear water afterwards: recently a valuable horse died mysteriously, and later death was found to be due to his having licked his stable which was washed in strong detergent.

The adult dog, properly exercised, rarely soils his kennel; and on the other days his quarters are swept out and the bedding shaken out and replaced. After the bitches have finished their season, we pour a pailful of boiling water down and wipe it as dry as possible with clean cloths. Rubber gloves for all these tasks, of course.

Remove cobwebs instantly: they are breeding grounds for germs. In hot weather, fill a garden syringe with a weak solution of pine or some light disinfectant, and squirt to freshen the quarters and keep flies and other germ-carriers at bay. If the dogs are resting in their kennels, a large old sheet, pegged to a line and kept damp (insect-repellent, again, in the water if you wish) will create a cool atmosphere if hung in front of the sunny side.

You will, of course, instantly burn or incinerate all soiled bedding and dirt picked up in the runs and exercising paddocks. If these are collected in a pail lined with a thick newspaper, it lessens the work and unpleasantness involved.

Kennels, Construction and Type: Ideally these are made of brick or concrete, lined-out with hardboard, with all edges covered with metal to prevent chewing. In all cases, have them high enough to stand up in, making for easier and better cleaning. Doors should open outwards.

If the roof is insulated or has an extra covering of roofing felt, no heat is lost in cold weather. The kennels *must* be draught proof and dry: our breed does not suffer from cold when in normal health; but draughts and damp are terrible enemies. Many a prize-winner has had his career cut short through rheumatism, and an otherwise healthy dog been condemned to a creaking old age, through carelessness in elimination of the cracks and crevices in the sleeping quarters. Never leave a window open above the dog's bench.

If the floors are concrete, you may like to cover them with Vinyl floor-covering, stuck down with the adhesive sold with each brand. This makes a clean surface for puppies; but they must have a large wooden whelping box where they can get purchase for their first staggering steps or they will sprawl and injure themselves. If the floors are of wood, we paint them with two coats of boat varnish, to ensure that the kennel can be easily washed and dried after any 'accident' or during the puppies' weaning period.

If the kennels are lined, with an air space between lining and outer wall, heating is rarely required for Shepherds – all they need is a dry and draught-free sleeping kennel, large enough for air and ventilation in hot weather.

Kibble (*see* BISCUIT).

Kidneys, Inflammation of: A painful and eventually fatal disease, known best as Nephritis. It usually occurs in older dogs, but young ones can suffer from it, too.

The primary symptoms are an excessive thirst, the dog seeking water anywhere all day long. There is vomiting and sometimes diarrhoea, and a very unpleasant odour from the mouth with sores on the lips. No meat should be fed, only white fish, egg yolks, some rabbit or chicken (boiling fowl) well boned, semolina pudding or porridge with plenty of honey; and dose with Denes Greenleaf pills. Consult your Veterinary Surgeon of course; but taken in time and put on a suitable diet a strong dog can live a long time without discomfort. Give barley water to drink.

Killer Dogs: When such a misfortune occurs that one of your dogs kills another dog, or a lamb or any farm stock, do immediately report it to the owner, who may well be wrathful but more inclined to come to terms and not insist on the death-penalty.

It is possible to cure a young dog of hen chasing or poultry killing by wiring a dead bird round his neck for 24 hours — and do not weaken, despite imploring looks! An unhappy 24 hours is a small price to pay for a long and happy life. Sheep chasing is another and more serious issue; and usually the only remedy is to remove the offender to a district where there are no sheep, and to keep him on the lead — always, and never take a risk, as he'll never learn.

Knuckling-up (Of feet): A well-knuckled foot is a great aid to proper movement, and an essential part of a working dog. Puppies should be put on to hard surfaces, concrete or cinder runs, or stony surfaces with some small rubble, so that they must flex their pads when chasing each other in play. At six months start the road work, only ½-mile at first; and watch that he is not over-tired.

Climbing up and down banks or quarry sides is also a help in forcing the knuckles into use, but not before 6–8 months old or you may widen the elbows and injure the front assembly.

Lameness: A lame or limping dog may be suffering from any one of a large range of complaints. He may have nothing wrong with his limbs, as sometimes earache or an abscess on a tooth, even a bad gastric upset, can cause him to move with a limp to express his painful condition. Rest is the usual cure; but if he cries when his muscles are tested, have him examined. If he is uneasy getting up from sitting or sleeping, it would more likely indicate a rheumatic condition, probably caused by lying on cold ground — dogs love to lie on concrete in hot weather! — or even a damp or draughty bed from an open window. So check all these causes as well as seeking veterinary advice. Two aspirins can give relief temporarily, but do not exceed the dose. You will, of course, examine his feet, particularly between the pads in case there is some injury such as a burn from treading on a lighted cigarette end thrown carelessly down.

Lice (*see* FLEAS).

Lifting a puppy: One of the worst experiences a breeder goes through is to see a tender, growing puppy grabbed and mishandled by well-meaning but ignorant applicants for one of the litter.

It is not always easy to prevent a puppy being picked up, or to read out or voice a list of 'Don'ts' before allowing the would-be purchaser

near the litter! However, try by example to show how a puppy should
be lifted by going ahead and picking one up yourself. Place one hand
under the hindquarters, so that he sits on the palm and the fingers
grasp the hock-bones firmly; and place the other under his body, just
behind the forelegs, so that you can control his front by holding the
forelegs and caressing his chest (*see* diagram). He will then remain

Correct hold of young puppy

comfortable and quiet; and should he make any sudden movement
you have a firm grip on him to prevent a fall or any pulling of a muscle.
Our breed grows so rapidly that novices often do not remember their
tenderness and proneness to injury during their early development:
a big dog at even six months is still very much a baby.

Lips: One of the ugly faults which detract enormously from true nobility
is a loose lip, giving a bull-dog appearance if really bad. There is no
remedy except not to breed from a specimen with this fault.

Litters, Size of: German Shepherds have such large litters usually that
one may be obliged to cull the family sometimes, to preserve the
quality of the whelps, and the health and future condition of the dam.

We consider eight to be the top number that can be properly reared
and cared for, even by a strong bitch with ample milk. It is better to
leave only six on a young bitch unproved as a mother. It is not necessary

to cull the litter until the 3rd or 4th day, by which time one or two may have faded naturally. Nature is over-generous, as the bitch in the wild state would have whelped down under a tree or bush in a burrowed-out hole, and several puppies would be suffocated or would die in the crush, or of cold if they were left on the outer side of the throng.

When your Veterinary Surgeon calls, about the 4th day after whelping to remove the dew-claws, slip any small or poorly-formed puppies which are unwanted into your pocket, one by one, or into a large towel, so that the dam is not alarmed or worried, and have them destroyed quickly and without suffering by hypodermic syringe.

In a large notebook put down the markings and sex of each puppy. This is helpful when it comes to the K.C. registration and for the information of buyers, although puppies frequently change colour and get lighter as time goes by.

Liver (for Showing dogs): Most dogs show better if rewarded or attracted by some tasty tit-bit. One that proves irresistible to most of them is made of liver as follows. Boil a pound of pig's liver gently for 20 minutes, and when cold cut it into small cubes. Place the cubes on a sheet of metal foil or a baking-sheet and bake for ½-hour at medium heat. Cool, and store in an airtight tin. The cubes keep well and are clean and easy to handle − a great advantage if it has to be taken into the ring in one's pocket.

Malformed Puppies: In a world already overcrowded with healthy dogs it is nothing short of ridiculous to try to save the life of an abnormal puppy. Ask your Veterinary Surgeon to use the hypodermic syringe on it as soon as possible: freaks are an abomination, and one should be glad of the freedom to dispose of them painlessly.

Mating: When a mate has been chosen for a bitch, it is customary for her to be taken to him at the date and time named by her owner in agreement with the dog's owner. It is a useful hint to give a small dose (a dessertspoonful is generally sufficient) of liquid paraffin the day *before*, so that she arrives with an empty intestine; bitches are often restricted for exercise during their heat, and may be a little uncomfortable in that region, so give her a little help. Take care to leave off all deodorants or sprays that discourage the dog for a full 48 hours before the visit. The average day for mating in our breed is the 14th after 'colour' has first been noted; but watch the bitch carefully − some will mate at 12 days and others not until 18−20 days. If you pass your hand over her croup with light pressure and she looks pleased and lifts her tail, taking up a stance, you may be sure she is ready. Whether she will accept the chosen mate is another question: most bitches are co-operative; but some may have ideas about 'Mr Heinz' who lives next door, or some other equally unsuitable dog, and be most unwilling to accept the male you have chosen for her.

A long strip of wide gauze bandage can be twice wound and crossed round the muzzle, passing the ends behind the ears to be fastened behind the back of the neck. This will prevent any mishap if she decides to snap at the dog, and will not harm her or cause her pain. Hold her head between your knees and talk to her gently while the dog's handler attends to the mating. Do not allow her to urinate or run about afterwards — put her back in her box, or the car, and keep her quiet for an hour, giving only a small drink of water if she is panting badly, but better none at all.

You will receive the dog's pedigree and K.C. registration number, also the Kennel Club's "green form" signed by the stud dog's owner as proof of the mating, on payment of the fee after a successful mating; and a second service free is usual should she 'miss' the first time. Always discuss this with the owner, as some dogs are heavily booked, and there may be some reluctance.

Meat: This is a dog's natural food; and although he can no longer hunt all day, kill and eat, and then sleep, his inclination follows very much the same pattern, and he is all the better when it can be adhered to as nearly as possible.

Feed fresh meat, as far as possible lightly cooked or raw. In most districts there is an abattoir, where reasonably-priced meat can be obtained. Skirt or flank of beef, ox cheek, tripe and beasts' heads — all are excellent for our breed, who thrive on all or any of them. Next comes the frozen meat marketed in slabs, which has some advantages but one disadvantage — it must be used immediately it is de-frosted; and in a small or medium-sized kennel this is not always practicable. Most of the branded meat products contain a high percentage of liver and tasty parts of the carcase. These are very good indeed in small quantities; but although they are excellent for many breeds, they are not suited as their mainstay to German Shepherds, which overheat easily.

Have a refrigerator for your dogs' meat if at all possible: it will save you much by bulk buying and avoiding waste through meat being fly-blown or spoilt. Failing this a wire-framed 'cage' of butter muslin, in which you can hang up the meat in a cool place is best. If you fear the meat has been contaminated by flies, rinse it in a solution of vinegar and water – one tablespoonful to a pint.

Tinned meat is useful as a standby or for travelling; but the preservatives and richness of it make it unsuited to our breed for everyday use. Nothing replaces the gristle and sinew of fresh meat for jaws, teeth and intestines and their proper development and maintenance. Such food also gives a Shepherd dog that hard-conditioned appearance that is so desirable in a working breed.

Milk: As with meat, the fresh variety is the best, and goat's milk when obtainable by far the most suitable. Milk is a useful vehicle for vitamins and auxiliary foods such as cereals, like barley-flakes and semolina, honey and some powdered medicines.

Skim milk is sometimes available and is excellent for puppies, inwhelp bitches and old dogs, as it contains many valuable properties without the fattening contents of whole milk, and is easily digested.

Fresh milk means farm milk, untreated. Bottled milk is not nearly so good so diluted evaporated milk is preferable. Powdered milk is prepared at a high temperature, which kills the essential minerals.

A little honey, melted in lukewarm water with milk added is an excellent restorative for tired or sick dogs, and is our major remedy for many small ills – also, all dogs have some last thing at night in winter. It keeps them warm and fighting fit, judging by the way they bounce out of their kennels in even the coldest weather. But do not give milk with bread or biscuit, as it ferments and is most unsuited to canine digestions.

Monorchidism (*see also* CRYPTORCHIDISM): This is a condition where one of the testicles is undescended into the scrotum. It is a disqualifying fault in Germany and the rest of the Continent, and a serious but not disqualifying one here.

Mouths: The mouth is the doorway to health; and bad teeth, sore gums or ulcerated lips should have immediate attention. If a tooth is broken it can tear the lips and cause intense pain. So have it removed at the Surgery immediately it is noticed. Sore gums should be swabbed twice daily with a solution of 1 teaspoonful T.C.P. to an egg-cupful of warm water. A small plastic sponge kept for this purpose is better than cotton wool, which is inclined to disintegrate, when small pieces may be swallowed. Any ulceration of the lips should be shown to the Veterinary Surgeon, as it may be a symptom of a kidney disorder which requires prompt action.

In new-born puppies, one should examine at the earliest opportunity for any malformation of the mouth. A puppy which seizes the teat with a strong sucking action usually indicates that all is well with the mouth. If milk oozes back through the nose, this means that deformity must be suspected, particularly a cleft palate, which will impair both sucking and swallowing action and the poor little thing should be destroyed.

Muzzles: A temporary muzzle for use while treating or attending to wounds, etc., or to prevent a bitch snapping if she dislikes the dog at her mating time, can be made by passing a wide gauze bandage twice round her foreface and crossing it; and then passing the ends back behind the ears and around the neck to fasten them firmly out of reach. (*See* illustration.) A little practice may be necessary; but

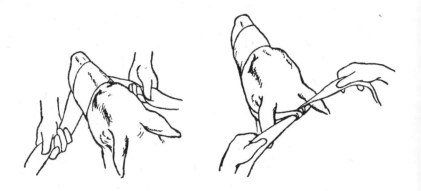

Temporary muzzle

it is soon mastered as an art and will save much trouble with a restless animal or one that is frightened beyond being responsible for its actions.

Nails (*see* CLAWS).

Names: All breeders of serious purpose have a registered prefix/affix which is recorded and paid for at the Kennel Club, and protected from use by others. It is only fair play (also, on occasions, wise!) to avoid registering a kennel with a name similar to any other in the breed. It is, on the contrary, quite acceptable and common usage, to use the sire's name for one of his sons — thus Dido of Exwood, by Dido of Wyewood; and I find it rather charming to use the names of famous ancestors a few generations later, and thus keep their memory green. But use simple names as far as possible, please! Pity the poor judges and fellow breeders who must copy out 'jaw-busters'!

Nembutal (*see* OLD DOGS).

Nephritis (*see* KIDNEYS).

Nobility: This is an elusive quality, yet instantly recognisable in a well-bred dog — the 'look of the eagle', as our American friends call it. It is the balanced dog, proudly carrying a well-proportioned head, at once quiet and well mannered yet having fire and drive in his movement — in fact an aristocrat of the breed, and something we all strive for in our breeding programmes.

Nose: Generally used to describe a trained dog's ability to follow the scent or trail — 'a good nose'. There are few German Shepherds who do not possess a 'good nose' — it is one of their strong characteristics. Dogs also remember perfumes and aromas attached to their 'dearest and best'. One of our Champions used to show perfectly in the ring with his owner outside, although she never attracted him by sign or sound — all she did was to puff heavily on the rather unusual brand of Turkish cigarettes she smoked: and up went his head, to present the picture of an alert, keen dog!

The nose as a nasal organ should be black, with large well-developed nostrils, cool and moist in normal conditions. A dog which lives indoors and sleeps by the fireside or a radiator may have a dried, even cracked nose as a result. Smear the nostrils well with Vaseline, in this case, and if he 'snuffles' at night, smear some Vick under his throat so that he cannot lick it, and the warmth will send up a vapour to relieve the congested organ.

Puppies sometimes have light noses, which frequently darken with maturity. A course of elderberry pills, which are rich in natural, easily absorbed iron, is helpful sometimes. 'Dudley' noses (flesh coloured) are faulty.

Novices: These are the experts of tomorrow; and no breed can carry on without new blood in the ranks of breeders as well as dogs. Most large breed clubs make a point of welcoming newcomers and offering help and disinterested advice; while if the stock for a new kennel is purchased from one of the long-standing establishments the novice can count on support and advice, and profit considerably by taking note of the results of the crossing of the various bloodlines within his new family circle, saving time and money. Even after years in a breed, one can learn a lot (if only what *not* to do) by 'lying low and saying nuffin', like Brer Fox.

Just when one ceases to be a novice is debatable! It is curious in a large breed such as German Shepherds, how a few 'old timers' stay the course over a long period and the breed remains, mainly, in much the same hands year after year, 30 or even 40 years' experience being quite commonplace.

On the whole, it is better to start at the bottom and work up, gaining knowledge and proving its worth by breeding a good 'un yourself; and nothing will ever thrill you like making up your first home-bred champion. It would appear that those who start by buying winners, and whose early efforts are crowned with enviable luck, do not come back and start again when the winning flush is over – just human, perhaps.

Nursing: Just as with humans, an expert Veterinary Surgeon, like an expert Doctor, relies on a good nurse; and a few simple hints may help in ill-health or after an accident and save a loved friend from a premature end.

A quiet place for the patient, where he is not distracted or disturbed by his kennel-mates, is the first necessity. A dog which has had a chill, or any respiratory disease, may cough and be restless. Give frequent small teaspoonsful of honey, glycerine and a few drops of lemon juice well mixed in to soothe and ease the condition. See that your patient lies well up from the floor and away from any draughty window; and have only enough light to see what you are doing – all dogs rest better in a darkened room.

Take the temperature according to instructions, if before the arrival of the Veterinary Surgeon, noting the time as well. In a busy household (more the rule than the exception), a small notebook to jot down all the facts, treatment, etc., should hang in the nursing quarters – memory can play tricks when one is upset or overtired through night nursing.

If the patient has gastric trouble, withdraw the drinking bowl and let him lick a piece of ice occasionally. Incidentally, ice-cream is a valuable aid in bringing down a fever and keeping a dog nourished. Plain flavour, of course, or better still, home-made with eggs and fresh cream.

It is difficult to make a sick dog relieve himself indoors sometimes. So be prepared to give an enema with lukewarm water and a table-spoonful of olive oil per quart of water added. This should be given from a gravity douche with the utmost gentleness and very slowly. Have a large flat container nearby with an ample supply of newspaper for the results, which can be sudden.

DO keep a constant watch on the poor sufferer, who will take strength and courage from your quiet, unflurried attitude.

DON'T allow visitors with fresh scents and exclamations to disturb and trouble him.

DON'T give human remedies without your Veterinary Surgeon's consent: you may do untold harm.

Obedience (*see also* TRAINING and Appendix C): Classes for obedience training are held over a widely scattered number of centres in the British Isles, many of them under the flag of the B.A.G.S.D., which specialises in this good work.

The classes do splendid work, particularly among novice owners; and many a dog's character has been formed, even improved, by his attendance at the local training centre.

Tests are held at many of the shows, and attract large crowds to watch the dogs working through a set of exercises for which marks are awarded by the judge and prizes given.

The repetition of the exercises in obedience work and the high standard of performance required and achieved, sometimes only ½-mark separating the first two in a class, has caused some disagreement as to the value of the competitions where a dog becomes somewhat automatic, even stale, doing the same exercises continually. However, nobody would deny that the fine work done by the trainers at the classes, in making the Smiths and the Browns control their dogs and enjoy doing so, deserves the highest praise.

Odours: A healthy G.S.D. has really no 'doggy' smell at all: in fact, a well-kept coat has a nice leathery smell rather like a new pair of gloves. But if the dog has some disorder of blood, skin or stomach, he may well not come into the category above, and as the advertisement says (in reverse) you must tell your Best Friend! *See* BAD BREATH for some of the possible causes. Also watch for one simple explanation – rolling in some highly scented place. We had a beloved house pet who secretly visited the rose beds at mulching time: and nobody could get within yards of her until the riddle was solved.

Bad odours can come from defective anal glands; and these should be checked and, if necessary, attended to by an expert, as it can cause pain if clumsily done. Check that the bedding is perfectly clean, too. We have sometimes found dreadful old bones or pieces of meat hidden away by the greedy: it only takes a few hours in hot weather for meat to putrify, and the smell is penetrating to a degree. A short course of condition powders or Milk of Magnesia will usually help a sour stomach. If any of the odours persist from the mouth or rectum, you must, of course, seek professional advice.

Oestrum (*see* HEAT).

Old Dogs: There is nothing sadder than watching a loved companion fighting a battle with old age; and as Shepherds live long (but never long enough) some extra care is necessary to make these later stages a pleasure for dog and owner.

Indulgence must be avoided at all costs. It is self-indulgence, really, as we like to spoil an old favourite, forgetting, since the show days are over, that we are harming him and shortening his life. As far as possible cut down on all foods: very little rusk, three-quarters of the former meat ration, and substitute fish with a couple of egg yolks twice weekly. Give a small quantity (¼-pint) of boiled Semolina (*see* SEMOLINA) and ¼-pint milk at breakfast, and the main meal mid-afternoon so that the dog can be exercised to encourage a bowel-action to make him comfortable, as he will doubtless seek his bed early (old dogs are great snoozers) and will be distressed if he has to break involuntarily the clean habits of a lifetime.

When the digestion is weak or the elimination difficult, we give at breakfast Irish Moss (also called Carragheen) boiled in milk and sweetened with honey which the dogs relish. It can be obtained from herb or health shops, or from Culpeper House, in convenient powder form. Yoghourt or sour milk is also excellent as breakfast, but not all dogs like these products. However, it is worthwhile spending some time over coaxing the dog to take them, as they keep the intestine clean and the breath sweet. Two Amplex tablets morning and night are helpful if the old friend is not so pleasant to be near; and a daily rub over with a damp wash-leather keeps the coat nice when old bones and rheumatism make brushing painful.

Finally, when the time comes to say good-bye, call in your Veterinary Surgeon without hesitation. Don't make the appointment for days ahead, and upset yourself; or allow the dog to sense that something is amiss. It is the last kind action you can perform for an old friend. So make up your mind, hold him and caress him whilst he has an injection of Nembutal, ask for a shot of Strychnine to be put into the heart to lay the ghost of the story of the dog which recovered after an insufficient dose of Nembutal – and go away for a day or two or visit a sympathetic friend, comforted by the fact that he cannot suffer any more and that you had and used the power to do this for him.

How often one would wish it were possible for some human sufferers to be given release so easily.

Outcrossing: This is breeding from totally unrelated animals, and can bring with it many valuable assets if the two parents are both of good type and construction – chiefly those of sound nerves and intelligence, since close inbreeding tends to weaken those progressively. It also brings the possibility of lack of balance and what may sometimes be called a 'bits-and-piece-y' dog. Nevertheless, it is a sound and worthwhile practice in a breeding programme if carried out with worthy specimens occasionally, remembering always the saying 'Breed in twice before breeding out once'.

Overbuilt: A dog with this fault lacks the correctly sloping backline and his hindquarters are higher than his back, giving him a heavy and stiff appearance. Many exhibitors try to stretch a dog with this fault in the ring, so that the back looks well in stance. However, as soon as the dog moves round the ring the high rear portion is obvious and cannot be concealed, however skilful the handler.

The root of the fault is in the construction of the hindquarters: the second thigh is perhaps too long and does not 'let down' properly. The back may be too short and level, giving a 'boxy' appearance without a supple vertebrae, which governs the action, particularly the hind propulsion.

Overheating: If the dog shows a tendency to scratch, particularly under the body and in the 'armpits'; or if there is any redness of the skin or small outbreak resulting from the scratching in that area, it is time to cool him off – many dogs become overheated in the bloodstream when changing coats or during a sudden spell of warm weather.

Cut out *all* starch from the menu and feed lean meat only, with a good dose of seaweed powder to provide iodine (obtainable from herbal remedy distributors). Give two condition powders each day for three days, rest three days and repeat once or twice if the condition does not clear up. No tit-bits, of course, and all the exercise you can manage.

Paddling: A term used to describe a heavy, threshing front action, where the paws are lifted by the pasterns and not in a sweeping, light action by the whole leg as a unit, controlled from the shoulder.

Paling Colour: Paling or fading colour is a minor fault, but one that should be viewed seriously, as it can so easily lead to the fatal Albino or White, which is debarred from the show ring and not even practical for a working dog. Rich pigmentation (and even in the wide range of sables, from iron grey through to soft golden, the tips of the hairs should be dark for preference, giving a lovely shading) with deep, soft brown eyes, dark rims and a black nose are correct for a quality German Shepherd, and any colour paling should be taken as a warning by the breeder. Grand Ch. Utz v. Haus Schutting was supposed to have carried colour paling; but he was so widely used that one could equally well blame any of the dozens of bitches he mated.

Parasites (*see* FLEAS).

Paws (*see* FEET).

Pneumonia: This usually follows distemper or a chill of some kind. If the breathing is laboured and the dog obviously 'far away', put him into a jacket (*see* illustration on page 43) and move his bed into the warm, having asked for a veterinary visit at the earliest convenience.

With the many antibiotics and perhaps an antiphlogistene pack under his jacket (according to medical advice) he may recover quite rapidly; but convalescence is long and tricky, so keep him quiet or with a quiet companion not inclined to tease or romp, and feed him with sardines, ice cream, egg yolk custard, beef tea jelly and other light foods highly concentrated until he is really on his feet again. Maintain a watchful eye for any relapse – pneumonia is dreadfully weakening in every way.

Poisons: If you notice your dog eating anything of a poisonous nature, push a piece of common washing soda the size of a hazelnut down his throat. This will cause him to vomit immediately, and perhaps save the situation.

If he picks up rat poison, there will be acute diarrhoea and vomiting, caused by the phosphorus present in most vermin bait. Milk is said to be a useful antidote, but call your Veterinary Surgeon to come urgently before giving this. Poisons have swift and, unfortunately, usually fatal action.

Dogs are extremely sensitive to strychnine; and an ordinary dose as prescribed medically to a human being may kill even a large dog. So keep any products of this nature well out of the reach of puppies, or others who like to chew when left alone.

Police Dogs: The German Shepherd Dog is used extensively the world over for tracking criminals, and also for police duties calling for the highest intelligence and ability, as well as for patrol work. It is beyond any doubt that by reason of their strong build, their weather-proof coats and their fine intelligence and extraordinary reasoning power,

Champion Roscott C.D. (Imp. N.Z.), grandson of English and Irish
Champion Druidswood Consort

British Association for German Shepherd Dogs Championship Show
1976. Busy scene in the dog puppy class

Typical head of young
bitch

Champion Sionhouse Pirouette by Sionhouse Ibila ex Sionhouse Desdemona, bred and owned by John Gossage (*Photo: Diane Pearce*)

Early contact is so important. This young kennelman is looking after his charges (*Photo: Sally Anne Thompson*)

Youth on four feet and two makes a happy combination (*Photo: Sally Anne Thompson*)

Druidswood Sapphire by Vikkas Tanfield Caro ex Druidswood Jemima, bred and owned by the author
(*Photo: Sally Anne Thompson*)

Sit—Stay! The well-trained dog brings great satisfaction to both the owner and the public (*Photo: Sally Anne Thompson*)

Champion Ronet Nina by English and Irish Champion Druidswood Consort ex Vikkas Ibis Av
Hvitsand, bred and owned by Mr R. Firth

Teach your dog to give your visitors a friendly greeting

German Shepherds are ideal for this work, provided their character is also right. It is hoped that every breeder will endeavour to breed from stock with sound nerves, and to maintain the dogs under conditions conducive to fostering and stabilising firm temperaments and good dispositions.

The title 'Police Dog' (P.D.) is obtained at the Working Trials held by the Associated Sheep, Police and Army Dogs Society (A.S.P.A.D.S.), the S.A.T.S. and others. Very few qualify, as the training is arduous and exacting and, in truth, not to be undertaken by everyone, as the trainer must be on a par with his dog in toughness and intelligence.

The Police Forces in this country are using home-bred dogs in increasing numbers with great success: many will recall the sensational arrest of 'Foxy' Fowler by a German Shepherd called 'Flash', a dog trained and owned by the Hampshire Police. 'Flash' tracked this man, an escaped prisoner convicted of robbery with violence, from the mainland to the Isle of Wight, where he was arrested. Exhibitors' pride knew no bounds when it was disclosed that he was the son of two Bench Champions – Beauty *and* Brains.

Pregnancy: A deep-bodied breed with plenty of heart room is able to hide this charming secret, and Shepherds are expert at keeping one guessing! About the 4th–5th week after mating the bitch will usually announce the glad tidings by her increased interest in food, sometimes after a short period of being 'fussy' about what she will and will not eat, due to the disturbance of early pregnancy. Her teats, too, will start to enlarge and swell slightly, and this may be the only sign until almost her whelping date, which can be in perfect safety any time after the 58th day following the mating: 63 is the official number of days, but there is no cause for alarm if she is a little early. However, after 64 days have her examined for any signs of a dead puppy or other obstruction: do not allow her to go past this date – it can cost you the litter *and* the bitch.

Her food during this period should be adjusted to the new requirements. Give a breakfast of boiled semolina with honey and fresh milk added (*see* SEMOLINA) or soaked barley kernels or flakes; and after the 6th week she will require her main meal in two portions. Give her one 3-grain Raspberry Leaf pill daily for the first month, and two daily during the remaining weeks – these are a sure help to a clean and easy whelping. See that she gets sufficient easy exercise in short doses – inactivity spells trouble when the litter arrives. Watch her temper, too – some matrons get quite 'waspish' at these times, and

she is hardly in a condition to participate in the battle she may commence. Massage the teats with a little olive oil near her date: it will
give the puppies an easier start. Do not feed calcium products until
she has whelped or you may have difficult deliveries due to overdone
bone in the puppies – afterwards she can be given this vital necessity
freely. Spoil her and pamper her, of course; but keep to her routine
and all should be well.

Premolars: These are the small teeth immediately behind the incisors,
or cutting teeth, and are frequently late making their appearance,
even coming through at 18 months old. Continental judges pay great
attention to their presence, and may disqualify a dog – even a champion in this country – for their absence in part or *in toto*. The argu-
ment against this would be that after so many generations of domestic
life and food the dog does not require the teeth for holding and tearing
his meat freshly killed, and that through disuse they are disappearing
– our fault, really, and not theirs! However, the standard says 'Premolars!' and we must try to conform.

Pulse: Although not so widely used as a thermometer to discover if
one's dog is ill, the taking of the pulse is an excellent guide, particularly when nursing a pneumonia or heart patient.

A dog in normal health has a pulse rate of around 88, but if he is
excited or has been running about, it can be very much higher temporarily. Take the pulse by slipping the hand inside the flanks: and
just on the inside of the thigh you may feel the pulse quite strongly
where the femoral artery crosses the inner side of the thigh-bone.
Note the rate and the temperature in a small notebook hung-up in
the sick dog's quarters, so that you may report to your Veterinary
Surgeon.

Puppies – Early Days: From the moment of delivery until they are
safely in the hands of their new owners, these enchanting, exasperating
and expensive Time-Wasters should never be left for long alone, and
require all the supervision and attention which can be given, even at
great inconvenience.

In a breed so expensive to feed and maintain it is seldom that a
litter (over the entire period of keeping the dam, etc.) pays a dividend.
But the breed must continue, and we all hope to produce a goose to
lay eggs of gold in the shape of a Champion stud dog in great demand,
or a bitch who has champions in every litter! In the interim, let us
concentrate on breeding healthy, clean animals of good type and
disposition, thereby providing many families with a loved pet even

if we do not always figure in the prize lists — we receive three requests for a companion dog of good character for every one for a future show dog.   Examine each puppy as soon as possible after birth and reject any abnormal ones.   When you have decided on the size of the litter to be retained (6 is ideal: 8 the maximum) note the sexes and record them in a small notebook kept hanging up in the Whelping quarters — all data should be recorded here, as it makes useful reference material for future use and one does not have to rely on one's memory, always untrustworthy when one is busy or harassed.

Quality (or Style): This is as difficult to define as nobility, with which it has much in common.   An elegance which owes nothing to over-refinement, and a strength without coarseness, with harmony and soundness are all part of 'quality'.   This excludes heavy bones, wide-set and over-large ears, loose lips, and soft under-bellies, all of which detract without being termed serious faults.   Small, round or light eyes and washed-out colours also can be called lack of quality.

Quantities (Of food — *see* FOOD).

Quarantine: In a breed which has its origin abroad, this is something of a handicap in introducing new blood.   However, there are now several excellent kennels open to take the dogs for the requisite six months, where they may be visited and tended so that they are not entirely strange to their new owners on emerging from restrictions. Puppies from a bitch which has whelped in quarantine may be released when weaned; and this is often done, although it is expensive and obviously carries certain risks.

Quarrelsome Dogs (*see also* FIGHTING): The Shepherd is not a belligerent fellow normally; but he is possessive and must be taught early in life to share his owner's favours and not quarrel with his kennel-mates.   A sharp word and a tap with a rolled-up newspaper are usually sufficient to warn him that he is doing wrong and displeasing you.   Try to give all your dogs the same affection, even if one does wind itself round your heart in a special way: even dogs are bad second fiddles!

Quarry Climbing: If you live near a disused quarry, or have permission to enter a working one during weekends, it is marvellous exercise for feet, and also for developing shoulders and forechests, if your dog can run and climb the steep slopes after a ball or stick.   I like to throw the latter and watch the dog use his intelligence in discovering the easiest way up or down, so it is exercise for the brain, too!

Quartering: A term sometimes used to describe the hind quarters, but even more often the 'quartering' or questing of a trained dog seeking the 'criminal' in the Police Dog test at the working trials.

Quivering: A dog which quivers or shakes should be put apart under close observation, as he may be suffering from chorea and need special attention – also a visit from your Veterinary Surgeon.

Rangy: A term used to describe a dog somewhat spare and short of flesh, which gives him an appearance of being of greater length or 'range' than he actually is when matured or in flesh and bodied-up. It is particularly applied to yearling dogs, which nearly always go through this stage at some time in their development.

Ribs: The rib cage continues back from the chest and shoulder, and should be deep and roomy with decidedly more 'spring' or roundness in a bitch than in a dog. The flat appearance is more noticeable than in other breeds, but it must not be slab-sided – a fault and untypical, denoting weakness.

Ring Manners: German Shepherd exhibitors are, generally speaking, a sporting crowd, and there are few complaints about lack of courtesy or consideration in the show ring – long may it continue so!

Always try to keep your exhibit from obscuring the judge's view of the one ahead or behind. Don't shout at your exhibit in the ring and distress others who are sensitive to scolding or make them wheel round when gaiting. Don't fuss and fidget in the ring, however nervous you may feel – nerves have a nasty habit of trickling straight down the lead to the dog. And *please* don't scatter tit-bits of liver, cheese, etc., all over the ring, so that others keep their heads down smelling these dainties. Be on time in your class, don't hold a conversation in loud tones while awaiting your turn to be judged, and *please* don't smoke in the ring – a carelessly flung-down cigarette end can lame a dog for many a day.

Finally, accept your position in the class with good grace and a smile: the judge has not asked you to enter, and if he does not like your dog (even if it wins under others) then you have what you asked for, his opinion, and you will know for another time. And spare a minute to congratulate the winner: he may have worked hard and waited long to gain a card in our stiff competition.

Ring Tail: A tail carried in a tight curl or ring is faulty, and nothing can cure it. The tail is a sensitive extremity, and an operation or manipulation in an attempt to straighten a hook or ring tail will usually only result in the poor dog carrying a dead (lifeless) tail and even losing the tip owing to the injured muscles and lack of circulation.

Roach Back: Sometimes called 'carp back' this is not seen very often here. It is an ugly fault, quite spoiling the lovely clean outline of a G.S.D. and having a detrimental effect on movement as it denotes a fault in the spine from which the carrying through and connection of movement are controlled and transmitted.

Roadwork: This can be tedious to the owner and to the dog, who naturally prefers to scamper free over heath and hill. However, it is essential for hardening the feet and developing hard muscular condition, unless you are fortunate enough to live in mountain areas where the dogs can maintain 'do-it-yourself' firmness.

Routine: Dogs, like infants, really prefer routine, although both enjoy an occasional break or treat. A well-trained dog will soon tell *you* what time he is fed, exercised or kennelled for the night, if you should be busy on other matters at that point!

The kennel routine where there is little or no help must, of necessity, be made to conform with the breeder's household duties. However, with a little yielding on both sides the gaps can be bridged to make smooth organisation. Have at least one good, well-fenced (chain link) enclosure, and put your dogs out early (7 a.m. is ideal): you are then free to attend to breakfast if necessary. Prepare puppies' early feed overnight, and give this at the same time. After breakfast, clean puppies and exercise adults. Prepare puppies' first meal of meat, etc. Clean kennels, attend to bedding, cook meat ready for adults. Incinerate or burn soiled bedding, and pick up mess in runs and burn it. Put the dogs to rest during lunch-time.

In the afternoon groom, and attend to special duties — ring training, show preparation, etc. Feed puppies and adults, and see that the latter are given an opportunity to relieve themselves properly — a short walk if possible before kennelling them when darkness falls. Adults should not be fed between midnight and midday, the traditional hours for digestion and elimination which should be uninterrupted. Give all dogs a brief run about 10 p.m. and a drink of milk, warm and with honey added in cold weather. Feed your puppies and the day is done.

Saddle Backs: Soft or sagging backs are often thus described; and as this fault springs from weak muscles or an over-long back it is very serious in a dog which owes so much of its beauty to the harmony of the outline.

A temporary softness of backline is evident in most bitches after a litter. As soon as the puppies are weaned, if the dam is in good physical shape cut down on her food, giving plenty of meat and un-soaked rusk for a while; and starting gently, progressively get her to take long walks and to romp and to run with her companions to restore the backline. Even if she is not a show bitch, she will be in better condition for breeding the following year if her backline is normal. Dogs with this fault should not be used in a breeding pro-gramme.

Scalds: In the event of a scald (or burn) the area should have an appli-cation of picric acid, which will soothe and heal. If this is not available, cover with a compress of cold tea leaves, bandaging lightly. A thick covering of tannic acid jelly is also excellent and we keep this available always, for ourselves, too; it has saved many nasty scars from burns. Give a tranquilliser tablet or an aspirin to ease the pain, and get pro-fessional advice as soon as possible.

Scratching (see IRRITATION).

Season (see HEAT).

Semolina: This is mentioned many times in preceding headings, and this is our way of preparing it. Buy a good brand of wheaten semolina, medium, not fine grain, if you can obtain it. Maize semolina, or 'polenta' is not suitable as it overheats the blood and makes soft bellies. For one average meal for an adult, sprinkle one level tablespoonful of semolina into ½-pint of water coming to the boil, stir briskly to avoid lumps and cook gently for 10 minutes (we leave the puppies' breakfast semolina all night in the cool oven of the Aga), add ¼-pint fresh cow's or goat's milk and a heaped teaspoonful of honey. Don't put the latter in the boiling porridge, as the properties in honey that are most valuable are destroyed if it is heated or cooked.

Shoulders: This is a point so complex that it is really impossible to describe accurately; and one must see a perfect (or near perfect) shoulder to realise how poor some are on otherwise good specimens.

Generally speaking we have good shoulders on our leading dogs, but loose elbows are the weak point; and these should not be confused with shoulder placement, as they are largely caused by poor muscular development and lack of exercise and are not, strictly speaking, a structural fault. A dog with a good shoulder may move badly in front having too swift a gait sometimes, as he has not a well-placed and muscular elbow-joint to control his action and give that typical easy swing.

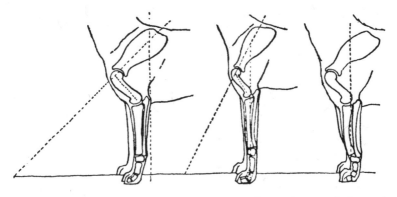

Correct front assembly   Front too steep   Coarse front with forward
*   and narrow   placed shoulder*

Showing: The exhibiting of pure bred dogs has increased considerably during the post-war years. It is both a sport and career. The majority of show-goers are breeders and many of them are judges, too, so that the shows are not only for the possibility of collecting prize-cards, but for comparing notes on the breed, viewing stud dogs for future use, studying the results of the crossing of various blood-lines and generally keeping one's ear to the ground to gather hints and news concerning one's breed. Approached with an open mind and a determined sporting attitude, dog shows can be great fun, having plenty of scope for the social side at the large events.

Much business is transacted at the benches and ringside with buyers who visit the shows, often from overseas. Thus, shows are really the life-blood of the fancy, and the ambition of most of us is to get to as many as possible in the crowded season from Crufts in February to the L.K.A. Ch. Show early in December!

Show-bag: Have a large bag of the hold-all type for your show requirements. For your dog a drinking-bowl (the folding plastic ones are splendid), his brush, comb, leather and towel, and the liver 'bait' or whatever he has to attract him in the ring. A couple of thick newspapers, rolled up, to spread on his bench are lighter than a rug, will not tempt thieves, and do not have to be carried home when you are tired. A small first-aid kit, with T.C.P., cotton wool, a wide gauze bandage and a miniature bottle of brandy should be carried.

Don't forget a packet of cleansing tissues for yourself and some good, easy-to-eat food — dog show food is expensive and frequently of poor quality; and the buffet is invariably 10 minutes' fast walk from your bench and has a long queue all day. I often suspect that the reason some people do not enjoy shows, or are not their usual charming selves, is hunger and thirst, as one is usually either blue with cold or overheated and longing for a drink with the bar over-crowded and one's class due any minute. Take sandwiches which do not create thirst and a large flask of boiling coffee with an apple or two for thirst-quenching. Add chopped lettuce or cress to sandwiches for freshness – a round dinner roll split, hollowed out and buttered, lined with lettuce leaves and enclosing a shelled hard-boiled egg is a handy meal and leaves no mess. Don't forget salt and sugar, also spoons.

Sight: German Shepherds do not possess keen vision like a greyhound. However, in common with most breeds, they observe movement of any kind from far away, which is the reason a sensible or enlightened stranger always stands still when a dog appears unfriendly: any arm flapping or running away would at once incite the normal dog to take action. While dogs do not (or rarely) recognise colours, they certainly know the difference between dark shades and light ones, many having a great dislike for white. Some people put forward the explanation that white has great luminosity and hurts their sensitive eyes. One dog I owned would grumble under his breath and refuse to come near me when dressed for tennis; and his delight when I changed after the game was really comic, so perhaps it's true.

Soundness: Accurately: healthy, right, hearty, stout, according to the dictionary; and this means straight limbs with no weakness such as sickle hocks, loose elbows or weak pasterns, and a good muscular development all through to ensure correct movement from the use of the sound limbs. Any weakness is unsoundness in truth, and must be penalised in a working breed which calls for health and strength as its hallmark. No dog is considered sound without both testicles – any lack of which is now a disqualification.

Southern Alsatian Training Society (S.A.T.S.): This Society was formed in 1926 by Mr and Mrs Leonard Nash; and they were later joined by the late Mrs Gil Hester – then Mary Akerman – who started breed classes for beauty and obtained Ch. Show status for these in the early '50s. The Society runs trials and a yearly Ch. Show for beauty, usually immediately after Crufts. The Secretary is Mrs W. Stephens, 20 Ince Road, Burwood Park, Walton-on-Thames, Surrey.

Standard: The Standard can be obtained from any of the breed clubs or the Kennel Club. It is the law as far as judging and breeding is concerned, and has the last word in all arguments and 'pet theories' put forward by those who would like something different to be accepted.

We must refer to it and use it faithfully, or faults will creep in and become accepted by novices who have never seen a German Shepherd as he should be without these faults. We must always remember G. B. Shaw's advice to 'get that which we love, or we shall have to love that which we get!' So novices should make themselves familiar with the standard of points as a correct guide.

Stifle: This is the thigh in ordinary terms, and much value is placed on the correct bend and muscular state of this important part of the hind assembly. It governs to a marked extent the elegance and efficiency of the hind action, and ideally is supple and in no way overdone.

Stud Dogs (*see also* MATING): Dogs at public stud must be kept in good health and condition as a duty. Do not accept more than one bitch in a six day period, if your dog should be one in great demand: it shortens his life as a stud dog and his interest will soon wane and earn him an unjust reputation at stud, whereas he is most likely only bored and tired out.

Show the amount of his fee clearly on his stud-card and do not allow 'arrangements', which usually fall through and are only for close friends or those who are working jointly on certain blood lines and have an interest of a special kind in the affair.

Spray or sponge the dog with some light disinfectant before returning him to the kennel, and keep him quiet for the rest of the day.

Tail: As the standard prescribes, this should be low-set rather than high, and hang easily down to just below the bend of the hind leg at the hock-joint. It should be bushy and have a sabre-like curve at the end. Hooks or rings are decided faults; but a slight hook with the tail carried a little to one side of the hock joints is permissible, although it mars the general appearance to some extent. A tight curl at the tip is usually caused by ankylosis – a fusion of the muscles.

Correct hindquarters and tail carriage

The tail is carried up and out from the body in excitement or when moving fast: but never above the backline to any marked degree. It is an unfortunate fact that many dogs with especially good dispositions have 'cheerful' tail carriages.

CORRECT TAIL CARRIAGE

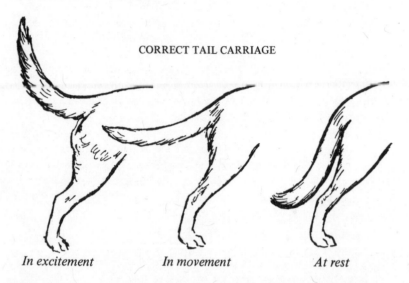

In excitement   *In movement*   *At rest*

Tartar: A large marrow bone, lightly baked in the oven first to discourage sourness or maggots, is a fine 'toothbrush' and should appear at least once weekly on the dog's menu. If the tartar is slight, or when the first signs are noticed, rub with a piece of clean cloth wrapped round the finger, dipped first in peroxide and then in powdered pumice. Swab the dog's mouth out with a small sponge and a weak solution of T.C.P. and water afterwards.

Obstinate tartar can be removed by scraping with the end of a disinfected nail file; but this is safe only when two experts can tackle the job, which dogs like as much as we do going to the dentist! A lacerated gum can cause trouble and discourage a show dog from allowing his teeth to be examined, so think twice before scraping.

Teeth: These number 42—20 in the upper jaw and 22 in the lower, where there are two extra after-molars. The premolars, 4 in number on either side, are sometimes missing (*see* PREMOLARS), which constitutes a serious fault in the eyes of our visiting judges from Europe. A missing or damaged incisor should be considered as a blemish only: dogs which carry stones, or even some which chew their way out of

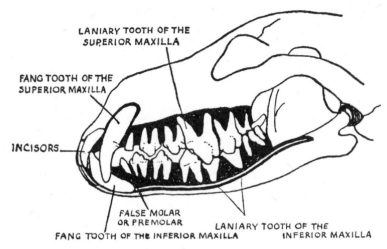

LANIARY TOOTH OF THE
SUPERIOR MAXILLA

FANG TOOTH OF THE
SUPERIOR MAXILLA

INCISORS

FALSE MOLAR
OR PREMOLAR

FANG TOOTH OF THE INFERIOR MAXILLA

LANIARY TOOTH OF THE
INFERIOR MAXILLA

Details of teeth and jaws

kennels or enclosures, often damage a front tooth, so this should never be classed as an hereditary fault.

Good teeth usually go with a strong constitution, and the result of correct feeding over many generations. The best kennels take pride in feeding their dogs correctly to produce good bone and teeth; and the wise novice will purchase from one of these establishments.

Temperament (*see* CHARACTER).

Temperature (to take): Buy a veterinary thermometer and keep it in the First Aid chest for ready availability for use. One's mind can often be put at rest by taking a dog's temperature when in doubt about his health. Don't forget that the sub-normal is as much an indication that all is not well as a high reading. The normal reading is 101.5°, but a puppy at 102° is quite all right as a rule – they run slightly higher when small and excitable.

Smear the end of the thermometer in white Vaseline, and insert it gently into the dog's rectum. Clean the thermometer on cotton-wool soaked in a mild T.C.P. solution before reading and again before putting it away. Note the temperature straight away – dog breeders have shocking memories!

Testicles (*see also* CRYPTORCHIDISM and MONORCHIDISM).

Training (*see also* HOUSE-TRAINING and OBEDIENCE): We have one of the easiest breeds to train, and there is little excuse for a dog behaving badly if his owner will arm himself with a little knowledge. Your puppy is extremely intelligent and sensitive, so take care not to spoil him: once learnt it is almost impossible to break a habit, so don't be over-indulgent because he is small and appealing, or he will soon be big and a great bore with his naughty ways.

Couple his name with the command, using as few words as possible so as not to confuse him — 'Blank — sit!', 'Blank — out!' etc. Praise and even reward (I am not a trainer and only try to have dogs acceptable socially!) generously when the puppy shows signs of understanding and obeying. Scold with the voice at first, and if he persistently ignores your command tap him on the top of the shoulders or over his tail with a rolled-up newspaper secured with a rubber band — the noise will have enough effect without a blow strong enough to harm him. Don't punish with the hand or you will make him hand-shy.

We find it a good plan to have him on the lead when introducing him to strangers. Make him sit and give a paw, and let the newcomer reward him with a tit-bit — this is an easy way to make him interested in visitors and not wish to run away and miss a treat. Training classes can be attended from six months onwards; but his home influence will always be important — he should be made to feel one of the family and take his place with nice manners as soon as possible.

Travel Sickness: This is a great handicap, and one of the favourite worries of the exhibitor. Most young dogs are car-sick, and if after a few trips he does not settle down you must help.

First of all, he cannot be expected to ride easily on the springy back seat of the car. This should be removed (which keeps it in good order for the back-seat drivers to sit on at other times) and a wooden platform made to fit the back compartment, with two legs on hinges which will drop down behind the front seats and hold it firm and level. On this spread thick newspapers on top of a plastic sheet, which will prevent any unpleasant happenings seeping through below, if they occur. A dog thus catered for can stretch out and is not bounced about, and usually travels well. Give honey and water to drink, and feed earlier than usual the day before the show or journey so that his stomach is empty.

Ask your Veterinary Surgeon for the prescribed dose of Vallergan — it varies with age and weight — if you have persistent travel sickness in your dog; and don't exceed the dose, or he will snooze in the ring! Tie a small Turkish towel, bib fashion, under his chin if he dribbles, or he will arrive with dark saliva stains on his front. Make an early start, drive gently, and arrive in good time at the show for any 'mopping-up' operations. A dog will ride better if he has an empty intestine, so give him a brief run first, even if you do make an early start.

Umbilical Hernia: This is a small (to begin with) swelling on the navel, due to clumsy whelping by pulling too strongly on the umbilical cord at the time of birth. If it increases or is visible, it should be seen by the Veterinary Surgeon, who will advise if operation is necessary. It is sometimes thought to be an hereditary fault, but there is really no evidence to prove this conclusively.

Undercoat (*see* COAT).

Undershot: This is the malformation of the jaw which projects the lower jaw and incisors beyond the upper (as in a Bulldog). It is less frequent than overshot (the contrary condition) and is a serious fault. Very small puppies having a 'grinning' expression should be carefully examined, as this is often a sign.

Urticaria: The appearance of large raised patches all over the dog is alarming and causes much discomfort. These soon disperse, and can be helped by applying calamine lotion. They are due — fortunately they are not frequent — to the dog rolling in some irritant, to washing kennels in some strong detergents without rinsing, or occasionally by food: the meat may be from some animal which has been 'physicked' with a product to which the dog is allergic. In human beings it is known as nettlerash and is not a serious complaint.

Vaccination: There are injections or vaccinations for many ills today, both human and canine; yet we still hope (and endeavour) to avoid a number of them by correct feeding and keeping. However, distemper, hard-pad and leptospirosis are still 'killers', and every puppy should be inoculated about the age of 9–10 weeks against these three bitter enemies — dogs living in towns or areas where there is a concentration of canine population should have 'booster shots' from time to time, on veterinary advice, of course.

During the interim between the two injections which make up the complete immunisation, the puppy should be kept on the premises and lead as quiet a life as a healthy puppy is willing to do. Keep a careful note of the injections given to each dog, as these sometimes have a bearing on treatment and reaction in any illness later in life.

Vegetables: Garlic, which is more properly a herb, is the best of this kingdom; and as advised under 'broth' and 'food', as well as its own heading, it can safely be given at all ages with great benefit to general health. We grow our own, as it is quite expensive to buy when one uses a large quantity.

Carrots are next on the list in priority, and are best fed finely grated and raw. Finely shredded young cabbage, raw spinach and lettuce can also be finely chopped and added to the main meal: well mixed in it will help a lazy intestine, and help a dog over his coating period, too.

Parsley and watercress are excellent for conditioning and toning-up a dog which has suffered a setback, either freshly chopped or the good substitute dried kind from the animal herbal dealers. Onions are inclined to inflate the stomach.

Verein für Deutsche Schaeferhunde (S.V.): The original German Shepherd Dog Club, founded in 1899 by Rittmeister Max von Stephanitz, the 'Father' of our breed.

This Club, with its system of selective breeding and control of judges and their training, has virtually sent the breed round the world, which still comes back to the homeland for new blood from the correct type of Shepherd Dog, bred and reared as working dogs within a selected group of tested animals.

The club's great show — the Hauptzuchtschau — held yearly, attracts an entry of some 800 dogs and lasts two full days with an interesting and absorbing programme. One of the classes which thrills overseas visitors most is the progeny class, when the leading sires parade with sometimes 30 of their 'get' behind them so that all can assess their worth at stud.

The S.V., as it is generally known, publishes a monthly journal in German. The Club's address is:

Verein für Deutsche Schäferhunde (S.V.),
89 Augsburg 1,
Beim Schnarrbrunnen 4–6,
W. Germany.

Veterinary Surgeons: Every wise breeder makes a point of being on good terms with the area Veterinary Surgeon who specialises in small animals — if possible, a member of the British Small Animals Veterinary Association. The profession is so spread out in its talents that each practitioner usually favours one branch especially — some even take an interest in one breed over others. So take pains always to find out which one is likely to be most helpful if you are in need.

We have had cause to be grateful for their devoted help and wise counsel on many occasions; but do not forget to play your part and carry out their instructions, keeping careful note of temperatures and symptoms (a small notebook hanging in the sick quarters is advisable) and calling in help in good time. Nobody can be expected to save a dog already at death's door after days of sickness without treatment.

Have a tablet of Canex soap and a small fresh towel or a roll of paper towels ready for hand washing. A cup of tea or coffee is usually appreciated, as meals are somewhat irregular when urgent visits have to be made early and late.

Vision (*see* SIGHT).

Vitamins: These are a necessary part of modern diet, but as additions to good food not in place of it. Do not expect pills and powders to make up for poor quality or inferior and unsuitable food. Try to give these valuable aids through the most natural sources possible — herbs and products such as olive oil and honey, seaweed and carragheen (a delicate form of protein). If you intend establishing your own kennels, you will ultimately reap the benefit of generations of properly-fed dogs, with good digestions and internal functions and no poor doers or rickety puppies.

Water: Clean, fresh water must always be available to dogs in normal health — some kennels have large pails at strategic places, while others prefer individual drinking bowls. The essential thing is that it should be there whenever required by an active dog which develops a healthy thirst.

Water, Barley: Dogs with kidney infection, constant or temporary, benefit from barley water instead of fresh water to drink. This is also very good for old dogs. Put 3 level tablespoonfuls of pearl barley into a large jug and pour on 2 pints of boiling water, cover and leave till cool, then strain and sweeten with honey or brown sugar, or glucose if advised.

Weaning (*see* PUPPY REARING Appendix D).

Weaving: This term is used to describe movement where the dog crosses his hind or fore legs (or both) when his gait is viewed going away and coming towards one. Over-angulated dogs and those with weak muscles frequently have this unsound action, which is untypical of the breed where the Standard calls for a firm, clean action with strong muscular control.

Weaving (or crossing) should not, however, be confused with a dog tracking closely going to and fro, this being normal, as a dog with a lengthy stride naturally moves with the legs under the body to maintain balance.   The hocks and shoulders should, nevertheless, not turn outwards, and the feet and hocks should move parallel although closely in these cases.

Weight: The ideally sized dog in true hard Shepherd condition should weigh between 75 and 85 pounds; but naturally, a dog fully up to the limit of the Standard will weigh more, and cannot be faulted for this. Only preference may be given to a dog of medium build which has a more workmanlike appearance.

Bitches, similarly, weigh between 60 and 70 pounds, which means that they must be strictly rationed after their litters are weaned or they will be sadly over-weight and lose on outline when in the show-ring.

Whelping: An in-whelp bitch should always be introduced to her whelping quarters about a week before the date when her puppies are expected. Try to spare her half an hour for the first two or three nights she spends in the whelping room.   Turn the light on, take in a folding chair, and read your newspaper or a book and chat to the expectant mother from time to time: it will give her confidence, and is the best method of preventing a bitch from anxiously hunting around for a nest wherein to deposit her litter.

When the bitch starts whelping, put her quietly in her room. Have a supply of lukewarm milk sweetened with honey or glucose available; a small notebook to jot down the time of the arrival of each puppy, colour, sex, etc. and any details which may concern your Veterinary Surgeon; and a tray or box with Dettol, cotton wool and cleansing

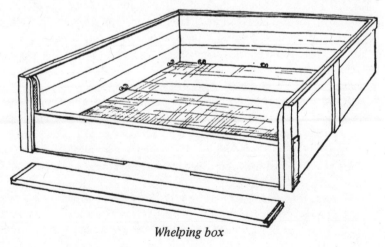

Whelping box

tissues, and a pair of sharp scissors which may be needed for cutting the umbilical cord if the bitch cannot manage it for herself.

If the bitch is comfortably housed in a box (*see* illustration) with sacking tightly stretched from the hooks, and newspapers underneath, it is a matter of minutes to change the bedding by slipping out the newspapers and replacing with fresh ones, thus keeping the quarters clean and fresh. When all is over, the sack can be replaced, too; but don't disturb her during the actual whelping — it may upset her nerves and cause her to treat her family roughly, even devour them. Offer her a small warm drink of milk sweetened with honey after each puppy; and when all is over, coax her outside — she may not like to go, but it is essential for her ultimate comfort and well-being.

Food is not necessary during the delivery of the puppies nor during the 12 hours following, although ample supplies of milk and honey diluted with warm water should be available for the thirsty mother. A packet of semi-sweet biscuits such as Petit Beurre is useful in the room to offer the bitch when her labour is over — they are light and easily digested. Boiled fish, carefully boned, with some milk added and an egg yolk or two can form her first meal of the day following, with a bowl of semolina (*see* SEMOLINA for preparation) in the early morning. Never give rice, which swells and causes discomfort. After the first 12 hours, if all goes well, gradually restore her normal rations, increasing as necessary to suit her requirements as her litter grows. Make sure that plenty of fresh water is always available, as feeding and cleaning a large litter is a thirst provoking affair.

Your veterinary surgeon will visit the bitch when her labour is finished to advise you if there are any dead or unborn puppies remaining. When all is clear, sponge her hindquarters with a weak solution of Dettol and warm water, blot dry with an old towel or some clean linen, and make her sit on a thick newspaper to complete the drying before returning to her litter.

German Shepherds are normally easy whelpers, but it is as well to telephone your Veterinary Surgeon when the bitch comes into labour, so that you know his whereabouts should his services be required. If left until an emergency arises, he may be away at a conference or testing a herd somewhere. So better to be twice sure than once sorry, and keep in touch with him in case he is needed.

Wolf: It is irritating to have the legend that the German Shepherd Dog is closely related to the wolf constantly related to one by ignorant people. The English are largely to blame for this, as the breed was first known in this country as the Alsatian Wolf Dog. However, since the breed's correct title of German Shepherd Dog is now in general use in this country we must hope that the legend is fading, so that we shall suffer less in future from the old misnomer.

Konrad Lorenz, in his wonderful book *King Solomon's Ring* gives a perfect explanation of the origin of the breed which gives the right answer to the man who cries 'Wolf!' Lorenz explains how most large breeds in Europe, including Great Danes and Wolfhounds, are pure Aureus (descendants of the jackal) and contain, at the most, a minute amount of wolf blood in their veins. The strong, individual character and reasoning power of our breed springs from the independent nature of the jackal ('canis aureus'), which is a lone hunter confining its activities to a restricted area, whilst the Spitz breeds ('canis lupus') hunt in packs roaming far and wide, and live their lives bound up with their own pack.

Worms: The most common of these pests is the round worm, found chiefly in young puppies, and which must be eradicated as quickly as possible since they retard growth and development, and also cause fits by worrying the puppy and weakening his resistance.

The safest way to remove these pests is by dosing with a fresh remedy obtained from your Veterinary Surgeon, who will prescribe according to the dog's weight. Remedies bought from shops may be stale, and often useless except to produce a stomach-ache.

Modern remedies do not call for fasting prior to dosing; but feed lightly the previous day and give extra olive oil in the food – also a small dose (one teaspoonful per puppy) of castor oil the day following and repeat the process in six days time. Roundworms lay eggs which hook into the intestine and hatch out despite dosing. Therefore to free the puppy completely from the pests, one must dose a second time to remove the newly-hatched worms which will not yet be old enough to lay eggs themselves. Unless advised to the contrary, feed a light meal of warm semolina or barley porridge after the dose; and keep the puppies under observation, for results usually show themselves within an hour of feeding.

Tape worms are found in older dogs quite frequently: country dwelling dogs which hunt or are exercised where rabbits run are often affected, and getting the nasty thing expelled is often a problem. Get the dose made up as for round worm, per weight: and keep the dog under strict observation after dosing, removing and burning all excreta, as tape worms infect and re-infect and are bristling with enough eggs to infect an entire kennel. It is essential to remove the head of the tape worm or it will grow again; and if in doubt, consult your veterinary surgeon as to the desirability of a second dosing. One has to be quite ruthless about the complete destruction of these pests, which will otherwise undermine both health and constitution and spoil a dog's chances in every way. Give a dose of liquid paraffin the day after dosing to complete the good work and soothe the dog's intestine.

Be ever on the alert where worms are concerned, and if in doubt obtain the dose for immediate administration: modern drugs are so easy in their action, and cause little or no distress, so no harm is done if it is a false alarm. 'Rectum riding' and general worrying of the hind parts are indications that worms may be present: also gaping, erratic appetite, foul breath, staring coat and a drawn-up belly.

W.U.S.V.: This is the World Union of German Shepherd Dog Clubs (Weltunion der Vereine für Deutsche Schäferhunde). It is on a national basis, with one Club (or one vote) for each country accepted into the Union. All countries have to be approved by the vote of the yearly Assembly of the Union, which is held on the day following the close of the annual Sieger-Show in Germany. Individuals cannot join, as many suppose, since it is the Club which is voted into the Union. At these meetings, matters of the widest importance are discussed on both the conformation and working side. Help and advice on any problem are forthcoming from the permanent Secretariat at all times, at the address of the S.V. (q.v.). The social side of the annual meeting is valuable, too, giving the delegates the opportunity to discuss breed matters informally at international level.

Yawning: Yawning (or gaping) is often an indication of the presence of worms, and should be investigated. A really hungry dog will yawn; and sometimes a sensitive dog will yawn from embarrassment if he is being discussed in his presence, or occasionally a dog will yawn from indigestion.

Yeast: This excellent aid to health and beauty is a good friend, but a bad enemy unless handled carefully. Brewers' yeast is wonderful for puppies and for a bitch during her period of heat. The famous brand of yeast tablets is also excellent; but care must be taken not to overdo or prolong the dosing by either method, as the substance keys up the nervous system, and it is unwise to allow this in a breed as sensitive as ours.

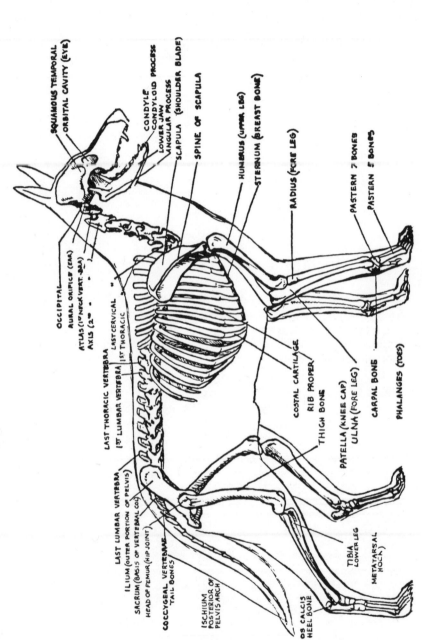

SQUAMOUS TEMPORAL
ORBITAL CAVITY (EYE)
OCCIPITAL
AURAL ORIFICE (EAR)
ATLAS (1ST NECK VERT.-2AA)
AXIS (2ND - ")
LAST CERVICAL
1ST THORACIC
LAST THORACIC VERTEBRA
1ST LUMBAR VERTEBRA
CONDYLE
CONDYLOID PROCESS
LOWER JAW
ANGULAR PROCESS
SCAPULA (SHOULDER BLADE)
SPINE OF SCAPULA
HUMERUS (UPPER LEG)
STERNUM (BREAST BONE)
RADIUS (FORE LEG)
PASTERN 7 BONES
PASTERN 5 BONES
COSTAL CARTILAGE
RIB PROPER
THIGH BONE
PATELLA (KNEE CAP)
ULNA (FORE LEG)
CARPAL BONE
PHALANGES (TOES)
LAST LUMBAR VERTEBRA
ILIUM (OUTER PORTION OF PELVIS)
SACRUM (BASIS OF VERTEBRAL COL.)
HEAD OF FEMUR (HIP JOINT)
COCCYGEAL VERTEBRAE
TAIL BONES
ISCHIUM
POSTERIOR OF
PELVIS ARCH
OS CALCIS
HEEL BONE
TIBIA
LOWER LEG
METATARSAL
HOCK)

Details of Skeleton of German Shepherd Dog

APPENDIX A

OFFICIAL STANDARD OF POINTS

Characteristics: The characteristic expression of the Alsatian gives the impression of perpetual vigilance, fidelity, liveliness and watchfulness, alert to every sight and sound, with nothing escaping attention; fearless, but with decided suspiciousness of strangers—as opposed to the immediate friendliness of some breeds. The Alsatian possesses highly developed senses, mentally and temperamentally. He should be strongly individualistic and possess a high standard of intelligence. Three of the most outstanding traits are incorruptibility, discernment and ability to reason.

General Appearance: The general appearance of the Alsatian is a well-proportioned dog showing great suppleness of limb, neither massive nor heavy, but at the same time free from any suggestion of weediness. It must not approach the greyhound type. The body is rather long, strongly boned, with plenty of muscle, obviously capable of endurance and speed and of quick and sudden movement. The gait should be supple, smooth and long-reaching, carrying the body along with the minimum of up-and-down movement, entirely free from stiltiness.

Head and Skull: The head is proportionate to the size of the body, long, lean and clean cut, broad at the back of the skull, but without coarseness, tapering to the nose with only a slight stop between the eyes. The skull is slightly domed and the top of the nose should be parallel to the forehead. The cheeks must not be full or in any way prominent and the whole head, when viewed from the top should be much in the form of a V, well filled in under the eyes. There should be plenty of substance in foreface, with a good depth from top to bottom. The muzzle is strong and long and, while tapering to the nose, it must not be carried to such an extreme as to give the appearance of being overshot. It must not show any weakness, or be snipy or lippy. The lips must be tight fitting and clean. The nose must be black.

Eyes: The eyes are almond-shaped as nearly as possible matching the surrounding coat but darker rather than lighter in shade and placed to look straight forward. They must not be in any way bulging or prominent, and must show a lively, alert and highly intelligent expression.

Ears: The ears should be of moderate size, but rather large than small, broad at the base and pointed at the tips, placed rather high on the skull and carried erect—all adding to the alert expression of the dog as a whole. (It should be noted, in case novice breeders may be misled, that in Alsatian puppies the ears often hang until the age of six months and sometimes longer, becoming erect with the replacement of the milk teeth).

Correct outline of adult German Shepherd Dog

Mouth: The teeth should be sound and strong, gripping with a scissor-like action, the lower incisors just behind, but touching the upper.

Neck: The neck should be strong, fairly long with plenty of muscle, fitting gracefully into the body, joining the head without any sharp angles and free from throatiness.

Forequarters: The shoulder should slope well back. The ideal being that a line drawn through the centre of the shoulder blade should form a right-angle with the humerus when the leg is perpendicular to the ground in stance. Upright shoulders are a major fault. They should show plenty of muscle, which is distinct from, and must not be confused with coarse or loaded bone, which is a fault. The shoulder-bone should be clean. The forelegs should be perfectly straight viewed from the front, but the pasterns should show a slight angle with the forearm when regarded from the side, too great an angle denotes weakness and while carrying plenty of bone, it should be of good quality. Anything approaching the massive bone of the Newfoundland, for example, being a decided fault.

Body: The body is muscular, the back is broadish and straight, strongly boned and well-developed. The belly shows a waist without being tucked up. There should be a good depth of brisket or chest, the latter should not be too broad. The sides are flat compared to some breeds, and while the dog must not be barrel ribbed, it must not be so

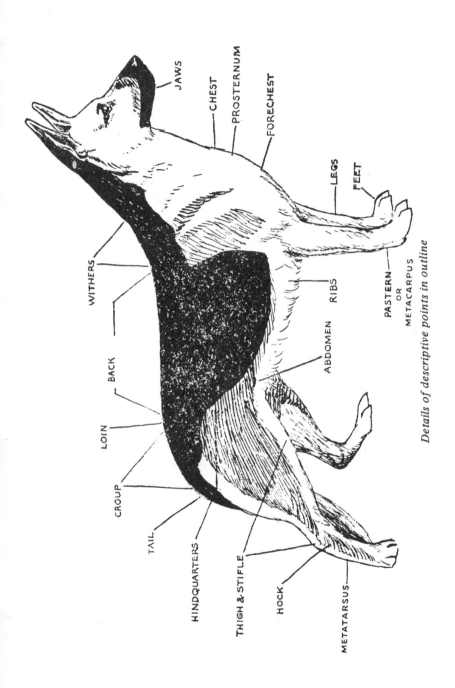

Details of descriptive points in outline

flat as to be actually slabsided. The Alsatian should be quick in movement and speedy but not like a Greyhound in body.

Hindquarters: The hindquarters should show breadth and strength, the loins being broad and strong, the rump rather long and sloping and the legs, when viewed from behind, must be quite straight, without any tendency to cow-hocks, or bow-hocks, which are both extremely serious faults. The stifles are well turned and the hocks strong and well let down. The ability to turn quickly is a necessary asset to the Alsatian, and this can only be if there is a good length of thigh-bone and leg, and by the bending of the hock.

Feet: The feet should be round, the toes strong, slightly arched and held close together. The pads should be firm, the nails short and strong. Dew-claws are neither a fault nor a virtue, but should be removed from the hind legs at 4 to 5 days old, as they are liable to spoil the gait.

Tail: When at rest the tail should hang in a slight curve, and reach at least as far as the hock. During movement and excitement it will be raised, but in no circumstances should the tail be carried past a vertical line drawn through the root.

Coat: The coat is smooth, but it is at the same time a double coat. The under-coat is woolly in texture, thick and close and to it the animal owes its characteristic resistance to cold. The outer-coat is also close, each hair straight, hard, and lying flat, so that it is rain-resisting. Under the body, to behind the legs, the coat is longer and forms near the thigh a mild form of breeching. On the head (including the inside of the ears), to the front of the legs and feet, the hair is short. Along the neck it is longer and thicker, and in Winter approaches a form of ruff. A coat either too long or too short is a fault. As an average, the hairs on the back should be from 1 to 2 in. in length.

Colour: The colour of the Alsatian is in itself not important and has no effect on the character of the dog or on its fitness for work and should be a secondary consideration for that reason. All white or near white unless possessing black points are not desirable. The final colour of a young dog can only be ascertained when the outer coat has developed.

Weight and Size: The ideal height (measured to the highest point of the shoulder) is 22-24 in. for bitches and 24-26 in. for dogs. The proportion, of length to height, may vary between 10:9 and 10:8.5.

Faults: A long, narrow, Collie or Borzoi head. A pink or liver-coloured nose. Undershot or overshot mouth. Tail with curl or pronounced hook. The lack of heavy undercoat.

APPENDIX B

Extract from Kennel Club Rules and Regulations applying to
Working Trials

8th November 1977

DEFINITIONS OF STAKES

When entering for Championship or Open Working Trials, wins at
Members Working Trials will not count.

No dog entering in P.D. or T.D. Stakes shall be eligible to enter in
any other Stake at the meeting.

All Police dogs shall be considered qualified for entry in W.D.
Championship Stakes if they hold the regional Police Dog qualification
'Excellent', provided that such entries are countersigned by the Senior
Police Officer I/C when such entries are made. Dogs holding this
qualification are not eligible for entry in C.D. or U.D. Open or Cham-
pionship Stakes, nor in W.D. Open Stakes.

No Working Trial Stake shall be limited to less than 30 dogs. If a
limit is imposed on entries in any Stake, it shall be carried out by ballot
after the date of closing of entries. Championship T.D. or P.D. Stakes
shall not be limited by numbers in any way.

Open Working Trials

Companion Dog (C.D.) Stake.—For dogs which have not qualified
C.D. Ex nor won three or more first prizes in C.D. Stakes or any prize
in U.D. Stakes, W.D. Stakes, P.D. or T.D. Stakes at Open or Championship Working Trials.

Utility Dog (U.D.) Stake.—For dogs which have not been awarded a
Certificate of Merit in U.D., W.D., P.D., or T.D. Stakes.

Working Dog (W.D.) Stake.—For dogs which have been awarded a
Certificate of Merit in U.D. Stakes but not in W.D., P.D., or T.D.
Stakes.

Tracking Dog (T.D.) Stake.—For dogs which have been awarded a
Certificate of Merit in W.D. Stakes, but not in T.D. Stakes.

Police Dog (P.D.) Stake.—For dogs which have been awarded a
Certificate of Merit in W.D. Stakes.

Championship Working Trials

Companion Dog (C.D.) Stake.—For dogs which have not won three
or more first prizes in C.D. Stakes or any prize in any other Stake at
Championship Working Trials.

Utility Dog (U.D.) Stake.—For dogs which have won a Certificate of Merit in a U.D. Stake. A dog is not eligible for entry in this Stake if it has been entered in the W.D. Stake on the same day.

Working Dog (W.D.) Stake.—For dogs which have qualified U.D. Ex and have won a Certificate of Merit in Open W.D. Stakes.

Tracking Dog (T.D.) Stake.—For dogs which have qualified W.D. Ex and which have won a Certificate of Merit at Open Trials in T.D. Stakes.

Police Dog (P.D.) Stake.—For dogs which have qualified W.D. Ex.

Members Working Trial

This is restricted to the members of the Society holding the Working Trial and eligibility for stakes is as for Open Working Trials.

SCHEDULE OF EXERCISES AND POINTS

COMPANION DOG (CD) STAKE

	Marks	Group Total	Minimum Group Qualifying Mark
Group I. Control			
1. Heel on Leash	5		
2. Heel Free	10		
3. Recall to Handler	5		
4. Sending the dog away	10	30	21
Group II. Stays			
5. Sit (2 Minutes)	10		
6. Down (10 Minutes)	10	20	14
Group III. Agility			
7. Scale (3) Stay (2) Recall (5)	10		
8. Clear Jump	5		
9. Long Jump	5	20	14
Group IV. Retrieving and Nosework			
10. Retrieve a dumb-bell	10		
11. Elementary Search	20	30	21
Totals	100	100	70

UTILITY DOG (UD) STAKE

	Marks	Group Total	Minimum Group Qualifying Mark
Group I. Control			
1. Heel Free	5		
2. Sending the dog away	10		
3. Retrieve a dumb-bell	5		
4. Down (10 Minutes)	10		
5. Steadiness to gunshot	5	35	25
Group II. Agility			
6. Scale (3) Stay (2) Recall (5)	10		
7. Clear Jump	5		
8. Long Jump	5	20	14
Group III. Nosework			
9. Search	35		
10. Track (95) Article(15)	110	145	102
Totals	200	200	141

WORKING DOG (WD) STAKE

	Marks	Group Total	Minimum Group Qualifying Mark
Group I. Control			
1. Heel Free	5		
2. Sending the dog away	10		
3. Retrieve a dumb-bell	5		
4. Down (10 Minutes)	10		
5. Steadiness to Gunshot	5	35	25
Group II. Agility			
6. Scale (3) Stay (2) Recall (5)	10		
7. Clear Jump	5		
8. Long Jump	5	20	14
Group III. Nosework			
9. Search	35		
10. Track (90) Articles (10+10 = 20)	110	145	102
Totals	200	200	141

TRACKING DOG (TD) STAKE

	Marks	Group Total	Minimum Group Qualifying Mark
Group I. Control			
1. Heel Free	5		
2. Sendaway and Directional Control	10		
3. Speak on Command	5		
4. Down (10 Minutes)	10		
5. Steadiness to Gunshot	5	35	25
Group II. Agility			
6. Scale (3) Stay (2) Recall (5)	10		
7. Clear Jump	5		
8. Long Jump	5	20	14
Group III. Nosework			
9. Search	35		
10. Track (100) Articles (10+10+10 = 30)	130	165	116
Totals	220	220	155

POLICE DOG (PD) STAKE

	Marks	Group Total	Minimum Group Qualifying Mark
Group I. Control			
1. Heel Free	5		
2. Sendaway and Directional Control	10		
3. Speak on Command	5		
4. Down (10 Minutes)	10		
5. Steadiness to Gunshot	5	35	25
Group II. Agility			
6. Scale (3) Stay (2) Recall (5)	10		
7. Clear Jump	5		
8. Long Jump	5	20	14
Group III. Nosework			
9. Search	35		
10. Track (60) Articles (10+10 = 20)	80	115	80
Group IV. Patrol			
11. Quartering the Ground	45		
12. Test of Courage	20		
13. Search and Escort	25		
14a. Recall from Criminal	30		
14b. Pursuit and Detention of Criminal	30	150	105
Totals	320	320	224

APPENDIX C

KENNEL CLUB REGULATIONS FOR TESTS FOR OBEDIENCE CLASSES

1st May 1980

(Reproduced by permission of the Kennel Club)

1. Kennel Club Show Regulations shall where applicable and as amended or varied from time to time apply to Obedience Classes as follows:

Kennel Club Championship Show Regulations. } to Championship Obedience Shows.

Kennel Club Licence Show Regulations. } to Licence Obedience Shows.

Kennel Club Regulations for Sanction Shows. } to Sanction Obedience Shows.

2. A Show Society may schedule any or all of the following classes at a show. No variation to any test within a class may be made. 'Run-offs' will be judged, one at a time, by normal scheduled tests.

Classes may be placed in any order in the schedule but this order must be followed at the show except that a Society, by publication in the schedule, may reserve the right to vary the order of judging when the entry is known.

The maximum number of entries permitted in a class for one Judge to judge with the exception of class C where Obedience Certificates are on offer, shall be 60. If this number is exceeded the class shall be divided by a draw into two equal halves, each to be judged separately. The prizes for each class shall be the same as that offered for the original class. No judge shall judge more than 60 dogs in one day and if a Judge is appointed for two or more classes the combined total entries of which exceed 60, a Reserve Judge shall be called upon to officiate appropriately. Show Societies should ensure that when appointing Judges for Shows sufficient numbers are appointed for the expected entries. The Reserve Judge may enter dogs for competition at the show and if not called upon to judge may compete.

Where a class is divided into two halves exhibitors who have entered for that class shall be notified accordingly of all changes or alterations and no timed stay exercises are to be held earlier than those advertised for the original class.

In Class C where Obedience Certificates are on offer one Judge only may be appointed for each sex. Judges must be present at all times dogs are under test including stay exercises.

3. *(a)* In all the classes the handler may use the dog's name with a command or signal without penalty. Except in the Stay Tests and Distant Control, all tests shall commence and finish with the dog sitting at the handler's side except in Beginners, Novice and Class A Recall Tests when the dog may be left in either the Sit or Down position at the handler's choice.

(b) Food shall not be given to a dog in the ring.

(c) In any test in which judge's articles are used, none of them should be injurious to the dog, and they must be capable of being picked up by any breed entered in that test.

(d) Spayed bitches and castrated dogs are permitted to compete in Obedience classes.

(e) No bitch in season shall be allowed to compete in Obedience Classes.

(f) In all tests the points must be graduated.

(g) Handlers may use only a slip chain or smooth collar in the ring.

(h) Every handler must wear his ring number prominently displayed when in the ring.

(i) The Show Executive shall appoint a Chief Steward, whose name must be announced in the schedule and who must not enter or work a dog at the Show. The Chief Steward shall be responsible for the control of any running order and for the smooth running of each class, and whose decision in such matters shall be final.

The Show Executive shall also ensure Ring or 'Caller' Stewards are appointed for each class scheduled and must not enter or work a dog at the Show.

(j) A draw for the running order in Class C at Championship Shows must be made prior to the Show and exhibitors and judges must be notified of the running order before the day of the Show. The Kennel Club will ballot for the running order for Championship Class C and Show Secretaries must forward lists of entries by recorded delivery or registered post to the Kennel Club for a ballot within 7 days after the closing of entries. Where a complete draw for the running order of classes other than Championship Class C is not made, Show Managements must ensure that at least 10 competitors/dogs are available by means of a ballot for judging in the first hour following the scheduled time for the commencement of judging of that class and these competitors must be notified prior to the Show. All competitors must report to the Ring Scoreboard Steward and book in within one hour of the scheduled time for the commencement of judging for the class and those reporting late will be excluded from competition unless they have reported previously to the Chief Steward that they are

actually working a dog entered in another Championship Class C or in the Stay Tests of another class. Where a complete running order is made, all competitors must be notified prior to the day of the Show and must book in on arrival at the Show. Published orders of running must be strictly adhered to.

Where timed stays will take place it must be announced in the schedule that they take priority over other tests, the times of such tests to be promulgated at the Show and published in the catalogue. In the case of Championship Class C stays must not be judged before 1 p.m.

Where Championship Class C competitors are required to compete in another Class at the Show the Chief Steward will agree with the judges of these other classes that the judging of such competitors be re-arranged in the running order. It will be the responsibility of competitors to advise the Chief Steward of the clash of judging.

In all Scent Tests, dogs should compete in the same order as for previous tests, but the judge may relax the running order where necessary. Scent tests must not be carried out during the main ring work but will take place as a separate test at the judges' discretion.

(k) Judging rings shall not in any circumstances contain less than 900 square feet of clear floor space and shall be not less than 20 feet in width except that for Championship Class C the ring must contain not less than 1,600 square feet.

(l) No person shall carry out punitive correction or harsh handling of a dog at any time whilst within the boundaries of the show.

(m) Judges at Championship Shows
   (1) For Class C at Championship Shows judges must have had at least five years judging experience and must have judged at thirty Open Obedience Shows at which they must have judged Class C not less than 15 times. Judging experience of other classes must include at least 2 each of the following at Open or Championship Shows, Beginners, Novice, Class A and Class B.
   (2) For all other classes, other than Class C, the judge must have had at least three years judging experience at twenty Open Obedience Shows and have judged Beginners, Novice, Class A and Class B each on at least 2 occasions at Open Shows.

(n) Judges at Open Shows
   (1) On first appointment must satisfy the Show Committee that they have at least two years experience judging at a lower level and have worked a dog in Licensed Obedience Shows and have also acted as a Caller Steward or Marker Steward working with the judge in the ring on at least six occasions at Licensed Shows.

(o) A judge of Class C at an Open Show must record in the judging book the number of points awarded to each dog with 290 or more points. The Show Secretary will record these in the official marked catalogue.

(p) The judge may allow a dog to be withdrawn from competition only on application by the competitor to the judge.

4. Imperfections in heeling between tests will not be judged but any physical disciplining by the handler in the ring, or any uncontrolled behaviour of the dog, such as snapping, unjustified barking, fouling the ring, or running out of the ring, even between tests, must be penalised by deducting points from the total score and the judge may bar the dog from further competition in that class.

5. *(a)* In all the following Definitions of Classes, First Prize wins in Limited and Sanction Show Obedience Classes will not count for entry in Open and Championship Show Obedience Classes. No dog is eligible to compete in Obedience Classes at Limited and Sanction Shows which has won an Obedience Certificate or obtained any award that counts towards the title of Obedience Champion or the equivalent thereof under the rules of any governing body recognised by the Kennel Club. Obedience Champions are eligible only for Class C at Open and Championship Shows.

(b) A dog may be entered in any two classes at a Show for which it is eligible with the exception of Championship Class C for which only dogs appropriately qualified may be entered. (Note the qualification for Championship Class C and Obedience Warrant).

PRE-BEGINNERS—Pre-Beginners Classes **may only be scheduled at Limited and Sanction Obedience Shows. If owner or handler or dog have won a first prize in any Class they may not compete in Pre-Beginners.**

Handlers will not be penalised for encouragement or extra commands except in the Sit and Down tests. In these tests, at the discretion of the judge, handlers may face their dogs. Judges or Stewards must not use the words "last command" except in the Sit and Down tests.

1. Heel on Lead   15 points
2. Heel Free   20 points
3. Recall from sit or down position at handler's choice.
   Dog to be recalled by handler when stationary and facing the dog. Dog to return smartly to the handler, sit in front, go to heel—all on command of judge or steward to handler. Distance at discretion of judge.
   Test commences when handler leaves dog   10 points
4. Sit One Minute, handler in sight   10 points
5. Down Two Minutes, handler in sight   20 points
                                                       Total   75 points

BEGINNERS—If owner or handler or dog have won a total of two or more first prizes in the Beginners Class, they may not compete in

Beginners. Winners of one first prize in any other Obedience Class are ineligible to compete in this Class.

Handlers will not be penalised for encouragement or extra commands except in the Sit and Down tests. In these tests, at the discretion of the judge, handlers may face their dogs. Judges or stewards must not use the words "last command" except in the Sit and Down tests.

1. Heel on Lead		15 points
2. Heel Free		20 points
3. Recall from sit or down position at handler's choice. Dog to be recalled by handler when stationary and facing the dog. Dog to return smartly to handler, sit in front, go to heel—all on command of judge or steward to handler. Distance at discretion of judge. Test commences when handler leaves dog		10 points
4. Retrieve any article. Handlers may use their own article		25 points
5. Sit One Minute, handler in sight		10 points
6. Down Two Minutes, handler in sight		20 points
	Total	100 points

NOVICE—For dogs that have not won two first prizes in Obedience Classes (Beginners Class excepted).

Handlers will not be penalised for encouragement or extra commands except in the Sit and Down tests. In these tests, at the discretion of the judge, handlers may face their dogs. Judges or stewards must not use the words "last command" except in the Sit and Down tests.

1. Temperament Test. To take place immediately before heel on lead. Dog to be on lead in the Stand position. Handler to stand by dog. Judge to approach quietly from the front and to run his hand gently down the dog's back. Judge may talk quietly to dog to reassure it. Any undue resentment, cringing, growling or snapping to be penalised. This is not a stand for examination or stay test		10 points
2. Heel on Lead		10 points
3. Heel Free		20 points
4. Recall from sit or down position at handler's choice. Dog to be recalled by handler when stationary and facing the dog. Dog to return smartly to handler, sit in front, go to heel—all on command of judge or steward to handler. Distance at discretion of judge. Test commences when handler leaves dog		10 points
5. Retrieve a Dumb-bell. Handlers may use their own bells		20 points
6. Sit One Minute, handler in sight		10 points
7. Down Two Minutes, handler in sight		20 points
	Total	100 points

CLASS A—For dogs which have not won three first prizes in Classes A, B, and open Class C in total.

Simultaneous command and signal will be permitted. Extra commands or signals must be penalised.

1. Heel on Lead   15 points
2. Temperament Test. Will take place before Heel Free. Dog to be in the stand position and off lead. Handler to stand beside dog. Conditions as for Novice Temperament Test, except that Test will commence with order "last command" and end with order "test finished". Extra commands will be penalised. This is not a stand for examination or stay test   10 points
3. Heel Free   20 points
4. Recall from Sit or Down, position at handler's choice. Dog to be recalled to heel by handler, on command of judge or steward, whilst handler is walking away from dog, both to continue forward until halted. The recall and halt points to be the same for each dog and handler. Test commences following handler's last command to dog.   15 points
5. Retrieve a Dumb-bell. Handlers may use their own dumb-bells   20 points
6. Sit One Minute, handler in sight   10 points
7. Down Five Minutes, handler out of sight   30 points
8. Scent Discrimination, handler's scent on handler's article. The total number of articles shall not exceed ten, all of which shall be clearly visible to the dog   30 points

Total   150 points

CLASS B—For dogs which have not won three first prizes in Class B and Open Class C in total.

One command, by word or signal, except in Test 2. Extra commands or signals must be penalised.

1. Heel Free. The dog shall be required to walk at heel free and shall also be tested at fast and slow pace. Each change of pace shall commence from the "halt" position   30 points
2. Send Away, Drop and Recall. On command of judge to handler, dog to be sent away in direction indicated by judge. After the dog has been dropped, handler will call the dog to heel whilst walking where directed by judge and both will continue forward. No obstacle to be placed in path of dog. Simultaneous command and signal is permitted but as soon as the dog leaves the handler the arm must be dropped. (N.B. an extra command may be simultaneous command and signal, but an extra command must be penalised)   40 points

3. Retrieve any one article provided by the Judge but which must not be in any manner injurious to the dog (definitely excluding food or glass). The article to be picked up easily by any breed of dog in that Class and to be clearly visible to the dog. A separate similar article to be used for each dog. Test commences following Judge or Steward's words "last command" to handler   30 points

4. Stand One Minute, handler at least ten paces away from and facing away from the dog   10 points

5. Sit Two Minutes, handler out of sight   20 points

6. Down Ten Minutes, handler out of sight   40 points

7. Scent Discrimination. Handler's scent on article provided by judge. A separate similar article to be used for each dog and the total number of articles shall not exceed ten, all of which shall be clearly visible to the dog and shall be similar to the article given to the handler. Judges must use a separate similar scent decoy or decoys for each dog. No points will be awarded if the article is given to the dog   30 points

                                                 Total   200 points

CLASS C—At Championship Shows: For dogs which have been placed on at least one occasion not lower than third in each class of Novice Class, Class A and Class B and have won Open Class C with not less than 290 marks on one occasion and have gained at least 290 marks in Open Class C on three further occasions under different judges. Dogs which qualified for entry in Championship Class C prior to 1st May 1980 are also eligible. **At Limited and Sanction Shows:** Open to all dogs except Obedience Certificate winners and dogs which have obtained any award that counts towards the title of Obedience Champion or the equivalent thereof under the rules of any governing body recognised by the Kennel Club.

One command, by word or signal, except in Test 2 where an extra command may be simultaneous command and signal. Extra commands or signals must be penalised.

1. Heel Work. The dog shall be required to walk at heel free, and also be tested at fast and slow pace. At some time during this test, at the discretion of the judge, the dog shall be required, whilst walking to heel at normal pace, to be left at the Stand, Sit and Down in any order (the order to be the same for each dog) as and when directed by the judge. The handler shall continue forward alone, without hesitation, and continue as directed by the judge until he reaches his dog when both shall continue forward together until halted. Heel work may include left about turns and figure-of-eight at normal and/or slow pace   60 points

2. Send Away, Drop and Recall as in Class B   40 points

3. Retrieve any one article provided by the Judge but which must not be in any manner injurious to the dog (definitely excluding food or glass). The article to be picked up easily by any breed of dog in that Class and to be clearly visible to the dog. A separate similar article to be used for each dog. Test commences following Judge or Steward's "last command" to handler   30 points

4. Distant Control. Dog to Sit, Stand and Down at a marked place not less than ten paces from handler, in any order on command from judge to handler. Six instructions to be given in the same order for each dog. Excessive movement, i.e. more than the length of the dog, in any direction by the dog, having regard to its size, will be penalised. The dog shall start the exercise with its front feet behind a designated point. No penalty for excessive movement in a forward direction shall be imposed until the back legs of the dog pass the designated point   50 points

5. Sit Two Minutes, handler out of sight   20 points

6. Down Ten Minutes, handler out of sight   50 points

7. Scent Discrimination. Judge's scent on piece of marked cloth. Neutral and decoy cloths to be provided by the Show Executive. The judge shall not place his cloth in the ring himself, but it shall be placed by a steward. A separate similar piece to be used for each dog and the total number of separate similar pieces of cloth from which the dog shall discriminate shall not exceed ten. If a dog fetches or fouls a wrong article this must be replaced by a fresh article. At open-air shows all scent cloths must be adequately weighted to prevent them being blown about. The method of taking scent shall be at the handler's discretion but shall not require the judge to place his hand on or lean towards the dog. A separate similar piece of cloth approximately 6 in. by 6 in. but not more than 10 in. by 10 in. shall be available to be used for giving each dog the scent. Judges should use a scent decoy or decoys   50 points

Total   300 points

6. The Kennel Club will offer an Obedience Certificate (Dog) and an Obedience Certificate (Bitch) for winners of 1st prizes in Class C Dog and Class C Bitch at a Championship Show, provided that the exhibits do not lose more than 10 points out of 300, and provided also that the classes are open to all breeds.

Judges must also award a Reserve Best of Sex provided that the exhibit has not lost more than 10 points out of 300.

7. The Kennel Club will offer at Crufts Dog Show each year the Kennel Club Obedience Championship–(Dog) and the Kennel Club Obedience Championship–(Bitch). A dog awarded one or more Obedience Certificates during the calendar year preceding Crufts Show shall be entitled to compete.

The Tests for the Championships shall be those required for Class C in these Regulations. If the winning dog or bitch has lost more than 10 points out of 300, the Championship award shall be withheld.

8. As provided in Kennel Club Rule 4(c), the following dogs shall be entitled to be described as Obedience Champions and shall receive a Certificate to that effect from the Kennel Club:

(a)   The winners of the Kennel Club Obedience Championships.

(b)   A dog awarded three Obedience Certificates under three different judges in accordance with these Regulations.

EXPLANATORY NOTES FOR OBEDIENCE TESTS
(TO BE READ IN CONJUNCTION WITH REGULATIONS S(2))

In all classes the dog should work in a happy natural manner and prime consideration should be given to judging the dog and handler as a team. The dog may be encouraged and praised except where specifically stated.

Instructions and commands to competitors may be made either by the judge or his steward by delegation.

In all tests the left side of a handler will be regarded as the "working side", unless the handler suffers from a physical disability and has the judge's permission to work the dog on the right-hand side.

To signal the completion of each test the handler will be given the command "test finished".

It is permissible for handlers to practise their dogs before going into the ring provided there is no punitive correction and this is similar to an athlete limbering up before an event.

Time Table of Judging—To assist show executives the following guide time-table is issued:

Class C . . . . 6 dogs per hour
Class B . . . . 8 dogs per hour
Class A . . . . 12 dogs per hour
Novice . . . . 12 dogs per hour
Beginners . . . . 12 dogs per hour

The dog should be led into the ring for judging with a collar and lead attached (unless otherwise directed) and should be at the handler's side. Competitors in Championship Class C who have lost more marks than would enable them to qualify with 290 marks at the conclusion of the judging to volunteer to withdraw from the Class with the judge's approval. This decision to withdraw is entirely at the discretion of the competitor and judges must not compel such competitors to withdraw.

1. **Heel on Lead**—The dog should be sitting straight at the handler's side. On command the handler should walk briskly forward in a straight line with the dog at heel. The dog should be approximately level with and reasonably close to the handler's leg at all times when the handler is walking. The lead must be slack at all times. On the command "Left Turn" or "Right Turn" the handler should turn smartly at a right angle in the appropriate direction and the dog should keep its position at the handler's side. Unless otherwise directed, at the command "about turn" the handler should turn about smartly on the spot through an angle of 180° to the right and walk in the opposite direction, the dog maintaining its position at the handler's side. On the command "halt" the handler should halt immediately and the dog should sit straight at the handler's side. Throughout this test the handler may not touch the dog or make use of the lead without penalty.

2. **Heel Free**—This test should be carried out in a similar manner as for Heel on Lead except that the dog must be off the lead throughout the test.

3. **Retrieve a Dumb-Bell/Article**—At the start of this exercise the dog should be sitting at the handler's side. On command the handler must throw the dumb-bell/article in the direction indicated. The dog should remain at the Sit position until the handler is ordered to send it to retrieve the dumb-bell/article. The dog should move out promptly at a smart pace to collect the dumb-bell/article cleanly. It should return with the dumb-bell/article at a smart pace and sit straight in front of the handler. On command the handler should take the dumb-bell/article from the dog. On further command the dog should be sent to heel. In Classes A, B and C the test commences on the order "last command" to handler.

4. *(a)* **Sit/Stay**—The Judge or Steward will direct handlers to positions in the ring. The command "last command" will be given when all are ready and handlers should then instantly give their final command to the dogs. Any further commands or signals to the dogs after this "last command" will be penalised. Handlers will then be instructed to leave their dogs and walk to positions indicated until ordered to return to them. Dogs should remain at the Sit position throughout the test. This is a group test and all dogs must compete together.

(b) **Stand/Stay**—This test should be carried out exactly as for the Sit/Stay, except that dogs will be left in the Stand position throughout the Test. This is a group test and all dogs must compete together.

(c) **Down/Stay**—This test should be carried out exactly as for the Sit/Stay, except that dogs will be left in the Down position throughout the Test. This is a group test and all dogs must compete together.

5. **Scent Discrimination**—A Steward will place the scented article amongst up to a maximum of nine other articles.

In a scent test if a dog brings in a wrong article or physically fouls any article (i.e. mouths it) this article will be replaced.

The dog should at this time be facing away from the articles. On command the handler should bring the dog to a point indicated, give the dog scent and stand upright before sending the dog to find and retrieve the appropriate article. The dog should find the article and complete the test as for the Retrieve test. In all tests, scent articles are to be placed at least 2 feet apart. Limiting the time allowed for this test is at the Judge's discretion.

Class A—Handler's scent on Handler's Article.

The Judge should reject any articles he considers to be unfit by nature of their size, shape or substance and which in his opinion could have the effect of converting this elementary Scent Test into a Sight Test. In this test at least one other article must be scented by someone other than the handler and the decoy article(s) must be similar for each dog.

Class B—Handler's Scent on Article provided by the Judge.

The article must not be given to the dog. All articles must be separate and similar.

Class C—Judge's Scent on piece of marked cloth. A decoy steward should not handle a cloth for a period longer than the Judge.

APPENDIX D

Preparation of the Brood Bitch.
Prenatal Care and Diet for Her Litter

When asked for advice regarding the breeding and rearing of a litter I always think it wise to warn the novice that it is not an undertaking for those with squeamish stomachs and that there is considerable hard work, also a great tie, when later on there are six meals per-diem to prepare and feed to a bunch of lively greedy puppies.

Take careful note of the exact date when your bitch first shows 'colour' at the heat from which you intend to have her mated; inform the owner of the stud dog so that proper arrangements can be made for her at the 14th day from her commencing date: this has been proved the best date for the average bitch of our breed. Now watch her excretions carefully and if any symptoms of tape or round worm are present, get a remedy immediately from your veterinary surgeon: she cannot have a healthy litter unless she is free from these pests. Exercise her normally; but it will be wiser to keep her on the lead particularly near her mating date.

The day before the mating, give her a dessertspoonful of liquid paraffin to ensure a bowel action early next day so that she will arrive with an empty intestine and feeling comfortable. This is an important point which is often overlooked.

Do not risk the results of lack of proper prenatal care by waiting until your bitch shows in whelp, start to build her up for the anticipated litter at once. Even if she 'misses' the extra conditioning will do no harm and is easily dispersed by hard exercise and a course of condition powders if necessary.

Give six veterinary yeast tablets each day and increase gradually to twelve by the 6th week and continue them until weaning time. Give her ½ pint warm milk with a teaspoonful of honey or glucose for breakfast and her normal afternoon or evening meal of not less than 1 lb. good meat, plus her rusk until the 3rd week. Now she requires for breakfast ½ pint of Semolina porridge, made by sprinkling a dessertspoonful of wheaten Semolina into ¼ pint boiling water and boiling well for 10 minutes, add ¼ pint cold milk plus the honey or glucose and cool well before feeding. Wheaten Semolina is excellent for bone and dental formation without over-developing them. At the 5th week divide her main meal into 2 parts; I give 1 lb. meat at 10.30 a.m., and 1 lb. meat plus rusk, 1 teaspoonful Olive Oil, 1 tablespoonful of raw grated carrot and soup at 4 p.m. A drink of warm milk when the dogs are let out at

10 p.m. is a ritual in my kennel, and this can be given with advantage from the mating date; don't forget to add a teaspoonful of honey or glucose—it is the gradual assimilation of these aids to health and beauty which are the secret of their success. At the 7th week you will want to divide her two main meals into equal portions, giving 1½ lb. meat, rusk, carrot, soup and 1 teaspoonful Olive Oil morning and afternoon, making the increases gradually. Do *not* give bones of any description to her from now onwards, and be careful of too much fat in her meat: the digestion is sometimes difficult at these times and she is already getting plenty of fats from the milk and Olive Oil. Don't feed her between meals however hard she may plead, her stomach and digestion are already fully taxed with her ample diet, and don't give baby foods or rich milk 'nightcap' preparations for humans unless you want 'podgy' puppies with spongy bone, also the risk of your bitch delivering an overlarge puppy: remember that a puppy of average weight is far more satisfactory than one several ounces over the normal 14-16 oz. at birth.

For the soup to pour over her main meals and later for her litter, here is the preparation used in my kennel for many years and which we call 'health broth'. Boil large marrow bones and clean butcher's scraps, sheeps' heads or ½ an oxhead with plenty of scrubbed carrots, two or three onions and several cloves of garlic for an hour, or more if the heads are large. Strain and bring the quantity you need to the boil before using, do not pour over more than required to make the rusk just tasty and crumbly. 'Sloppy' food makes for dirty teeth and sour stomachs. You must dilute it with boiling water for the puppies at first, although they quickly get accustomed to these natural foods. Weak hot Marmite may be used if one is ever without broth, but it is too salty for regular use. Keep the unused soup in the refrigerator, or scald it each day to keep it sweet and make it freshly every 4 or 5 days.

A week before the bitch is due to whelp, introduce her to her maternity home and feed her there in the afternoon and evening so that she feels at ease and comfortable; at this time give her daily a gentle massage of the teats with Olive Oil, this helps make them supple and prevents cracking and soreness in maidens. Don't be alarmed if a few drops of milk appear about the 59th day: this is normal and your bitch may now go down at any time in perfect safety.

At this period your expectant mother may go off her food or become very 'choice' about what she wants to eat, so feed her what she likes best and will eat readily, a little cooked meat or boiled white fish with some rusk, an egg beaten up in warm milk, and a barley flakes pudding, always with the invaluable honey (the imported kind is good and cheap). Many bitches eat normally right up to whelping, but one must always be prepared to pamper them for the last day or two.

The actual whelping down (always a wonderful experience) is for another chapter, but do give her small and frequent quantities of warm milk, glucose and also calcium, now and forthwith, a teaspoonful of the granular kind or one tablet crushed thoroughly in each of her milk feeds during her labour. If fresh untreated milk or goat's milk is not available, substitute evaporated milk (*See* MILK.)

No meat or fish on this day or the following after whelping. Give milk with honey or glucose and calcium as above, barley pudding and Semolina porridge and some kind of sweet biscuits of the plainer kind such as digestive or petit beurre: these are easily digested and usually readily taken by the busy mother.

The 3rd day, if all goes well, feed one meal of cooked lean meat and one of boiled white fish with rusk, etc. Do not make these sloppy with too much soup, and give the mother milk and water with honey in half and half proportions and in half pint quantities every two hours beginning at 7 a.m. until 11 p.m.—she will appreciate this for the first few days only. Now you will be fully occupied as she should have her early warm drink, then her breakfast of Semolina about 8 a.m.; 1–1½ lb. cooked meat, rusk, carrot and Olive Oil at 10.30 a.m. Pint milk and honey at 2 p.m., another ration similar to the morning meal at 4 p.m. Pint milk and honey at 7 p.m. and again at 10 p.m. with a few sweet biscuits.

Do put the dose of calcium recommended previously in each milk or pudding feed.

Naturally with such a large intake of liquids she will want to go out frequently, so please *do* encourage her outside to make herself comfortable. Most bitches refuse to do this in the whelping kennel, and it is not difficult to imagine the distress and harm caused by an overburdened bladder or bowel.

Now the puppies are two or three days old you must remember to have the hind dew-claws removed, either by your veterinary surgeon or an expert, so as to prevent both distress and possible future disfiguration by a clumsy operation.

At 14 days start your puppies on meat, this being their most natural food.

Carefully pulp, on a clean board and with a heavy knife, some choice pieces of meat and scrupulously remove all fat and sinew. Take up a puppy and insert gently a scrap of meat on the tip of your little finger, into its mouth. Some puppies will attempt to devour the meat and your finger too, others are slower and 'mouth' the meat for the first few times: that is why it is advisable to start early so that by the time they really need the protein they are taking it willingly in sufficient quantities.

Put them back on their dam as soon as they have all tasted their new diet, this will help them to digest it. Work up to a full teaspoonful in two or three days, given once daily, then twice daily until the beginning of the fourth week. During this important week they should start to lap, so begin by placing a flat plate or dish half filled with warm milk and water well sweetened with glucose, on the clean floor where there is neither bedding nor sawdust; group your puppies round the dish, dip your fingers in the milk and then put them in their mouths to encourage them to drink. After a daily sample for two or three days they will lap quite well, but one must be patient and be prepared to give them plenty of time. Personally I enjoy these early contacts with the little things best of all. Gentle handling and care at this age are an enormous help to the puppies' character and development. A well-known doctor on his round of a children's ward once wrote on the chart of a puny and backward infant, 'This baby to be loved every two hours' and so it is with puppies, they need fondling and care to develop the lovely characteristic companion-to-man nature of our breed and it helps sturdy growth when they sense that they are in understanding hands.

To those who argue that this is unnatural, I would reply that the little things are born under domestic circumstances, so must be reared to take their place in our restricted existence, and will never roam wild to seek their meat by hunting, more's the pity perhaps!

One other thing that must be done during this week is to gently snip off with a sharp pair of blunt-ended scissors, the tiny white tips of the puppies' claws which will begin now to tear at their dam's teats and the surrounding tender area.

Here we are at the fifth week and your litter will be eating, by gradual daily increases, 1 dessertspoonful pulped meat twice daily and lapping 2oz. (4 oz. with water) milk and glucose, also twice daily.

Now we begin their cereal food. *Wholemeal* bread crumbs dried in a cool oven after baking is finished, with the door ajar, or on top of the hot water tank all night on a flat tin (we save the crumbs from our home-made wholemeal rusk) are moistened with hot milk in the proportion of ¼ pint to a heaped tablespoonful of crumbs. Leave to soak and swell a little, add a little honey (or if you are self-sacrificing, brown sugar!) and introduce the puppies to this as you did the meat. The next day scald the crumbs with diluted 'health broth' and mix it well with the pulped meat and feed as usual twice daily gradually increasing the quantities so that by the sixth week they are eating as follows: Two meals of 1 tablespoonful soaked crumbs and one heaped tablespoonful pulped meat per puppy, 2 meals of 3 oz. milk, 1 oz. water and ½ teaspoonful honey or glucose per puppy. This is the time to start them on Semolina and barley flakes, cook the porridge as for the mother allowing ¼ pint water and 1 dessertspoonful Semolina between two puppies, add milk in the same proportion with one teaspoonful honey, glucose or brown sugar for each puppy. Barley flakes or kernels can be made in the same way or cooked as a pudding in the oven for ½ hour but it takes longer to cool, and care must always be taken not to give food too hot as this can cause much pain and damage to tender little mouths and throats.

You are now at the beginning of the sixth week and can establish a regular progressive feeding plan; you will find the litter all ready and eager for their meals if you take their dam away from them at least 1 hour before feeding times. If you notice any continued 'scouring' amongst the puppies, they can be given ½ teaspoonful of milk of magnesia to correct acidity, without detriment at this age. During this week you must begin to decrease the mother's ration, stop the breakfast by degrees, giving the milk drink only and cut down the meat and rusk until she is having 1 lb. at each meal, and finally give a warm milk drink at bedtime. The puppies will be nearly self-supporting by the sixth week, their dam will be weary of them and want to keep the nourishment to regain her own strength, so if she nurses them 3 or 4 times during the day at this juncture (especially early and last thing at night) she will be doing her duty nicely: however, you must arrange the sleeping accommodation so that she can get in and out (or up and down) to her family, so that she has her rest away from their torments. We have a slide about 2 ft. high fitted into the doorway and a comfortable bed for mother in the enclosure outside the whelping kennel; but where this is not convenient a bench high enough to allow a nursing bitch to jump on to it easily, should be placed inside the kennel. Cut the puppies claw tips again.

With your litter a full six weeks old it is time to give them the first and all important worming for round worms. Order the remedy from your veterinary surgeon, telling him the breed and age of the puppies, then for three days before dosing give one teaspoonful of liquid paraffin to each puppy (they usually like this and will lick it off a large spoon) every day and on the 3rd day, bread and milk and bread and broth only. Dose early in the morning of the 4th day, and watch for the results, clearing the run or kennel frequently. The following day give each a teaspoonful of castor oil—and repeat the whole performance one week later. It is impossible for a puppy to thrive properly unless it is free from round worms, and all your care and attention and the good food will be wasted unless this task is scrupulously carried out.

Their diet from now on, with the dam only giving them a little 'nightcap' until the end of the week should be as follows: breakfast at 7.30 a.m. ¼ pint Semolina porridge, ¼ pint fresh milk, 1 calcium tablet crushed finely (or one tablespoonful granular), one teaspoonful honey, glucose or brown sugar per puppy; 10.30, ¼ lb. finely minced meat, 2 heaped tablespoonfuls crumbs, 4 drops Olive Oil, 1 teaspoonful finely grated carrot, 2-3 tablespoonfuls boiling 'health broth'; 2 p.m., ½ pint warm milk with calcium and honey as at breakfast; 4 p.m. same as 10.30 a.m.; 7 p.m. same as 2 p.m.; and at 10 p.m. Semolina or barley flakes as at breakfast, with a hard well rusked brown crust to chew in their sleeping box, excellent for teeth and as a plaything so that they settle quietly for the night. A large well-boiled marrow bone from the soup can be given 2 or 3 times per week, not more often as bones are constipating. All these quantities are for the end of the week and *must* be worked up to gradually. Also when commencing the minced up meat it should be done with a fine cutter and from choice pieces only with no skin or gristle or excess of fat.

Now that the mother has completed her nursing period it is a good plan to give her teats a daily massage with a mixture of half olive oil and half methylated spirits. This has the dual advantage of drying off the milk supply and returning your bitch to her show career looking like a maiden. Do this for a week or until she looks normal.

Cut out all her milk feeds now, too, and give her 2 condition powders each morning for 3-4 days and feed plenty of meat and an egg each day for a week or two to help her back to normal.

You may like to cut the puppies' claw tips for a 3rd time about now, it will help them to have nice rounded feet later on if the claws are kept short now. After a busy week with dam and litter you should start their 8th week by the first increase towards 10 oz. meat per day and give more crumbs in proportion, too, whilst changing over to wholemeal bread cut into tiny cubes and well rusked as for crumbs. We make our supply 2-3 times weekly and keep it in a large airtight tin.

9th week. Increase meat to 12 oz., increase rusk, decrease and stop 7 p m, milk feed by the end of the week. Increase Olive Oil to ½ teaspoonful on each main meal and begin veterinary yeast tablets, 2 each per day working up to 6 per day by the 10th week.

10th week. Increase the meat to 1 lb. per day and give them as much wholemeal rusk as they will clear up readily, taking care not to make it too soft when adding the soup: chewing is good for the teeth and jaw development. Cut the rusk larger now, in cubes about 1 in. square.

At 3 months, worm your puppy (puppies) again, and he should now be eating 1¼-1½ lb. meat, half the quantity at each of the main meals, all the rusk he will eat, 2 teaspoonsful Olive Oil, 6 yeast tablets and 4 calcium tablets (in his milk feeds) per day. You can now decrease and stop the 2 o'clock milk feed and this will be his diet until 6 months when the cereal feed at bedtime is gradually discontinued and a small drink of warm milk with his honey and calcium is given instead. Continue the breakfast cereal until he is one year old and longer if he needs further bodying up, and watch his excretions for signs of worms.

See that there is always plenty of clean drinking water available for your puppies, as they tend to play with water and the drinking receptacles. We make a point of offering a drink at mealtimes and every time they are attended to, cleaned out, etc., about a dozen times during the day in total, until they learn to behave and drink like the adults.

With all young stock there is nothing to equal 'the eye of the master' so try to be with your puppies as much as possible, or leave them only with a responsible trained person. You will probably find, as I always do, that you will hate to miss a day of their intriguing antics, and once their routine is established one doesn't notice the work; in any case it is far less trouble than coping with sickly puppies making poor progress later as a result of defective diet and lack of attention.

Make all the increases and decreases *gradually* and watch your litter at mealtimes, checking the over-greedy and feeding a slow eater separately if necessary until he catches up with the others.

Small doses (a teaspoonful to a dessertspoonful) of milk of magnesia can be given if they seem to have internal disturbance due to teething or the change of diet: it is most helpful in minor digestive ailments; but if there is prolonged disorder you must call in the veterinary surgeon.

Keep your puppies dry and reasonably warm: our breed do not need heating except in unusually cold weather, but they *must* be kept out of the damp and draughts.

GLOSSARY

Short Glossary of German descriptive terms, useful when reading German stud-books or the pedigrees of imported dogs.

ABZEICHEN (A): Markings
AHNEN: Ancestors
AHNENTAFEL: Pedigree
ALLGEMEINE ERSCHEINUNG:
    General appearance
ALTER: Age
ALTERKLASSE (AK): Adult class
ANGEKÖRT: Certified suitable
    for breeding
AUGEN: Eyes
AUSDRUCK: Character
BAUCH: Belly
BEFRIEDIGEND (B): Fair
BEHAARUNG: Coat
BELEGT: Bred
BESITZER: Owner
BEWERTUNG: Qualification
BLAU: Blue-grey
BRAUN: Brown
BREIT: Broad
BRUST (BR): Chest
DECKFARBE: Predominant Colour
DRAHTHAARIG: Wire coated
DUNKEL (D): Dark
EHRENPREIS: Prize of Honour
ELTERN: Parents
ENG: Narrow
ENKEL, ENKELIN:
    Grandson, Granddaughter
ERZIEHUNG:
    Upbringing, Training
FARBE: Colour
FASSBEINE: Bowlegged

FASSRIPPE: Barrel-ribbed
FLANKE: Loin
FLUCHTIG: Fleet
FUTTERZUSTAND: Fine Condition
GANG: Gait
GELB (G): Gold
GELBGRAU: Tan/grey sable
GESCHLECHTSGEPRÄGE:
    Sex-quality
GESUNDHEIT: Sound health
GEWOLKT: Dingy, mixed colours
GEWINKELT: Angulated
GEWORFEN: Whelped
GLATTERHAARIG: Smooth coated
GRAUGELB: Greyish tan (sable)
GROSS: Large
GROSSELTERN: Grandparents
GUT (G): Good
HALS: Throat, neck
HARMONISCH: Co-ordinated
HART: Hard
HASENFUSS: Hare-foot(ed)
HELL: Light colour
HINTERBEINE: Hind legs
HOCKE: Hock
HODEN: Testicles
HOHE: Height
HUND (R): Dog
HÜNDIN (H): Bitch
JUGEND: Youth
JUGENDKLASSE (J.K.): Youth class
JUNGHUND: Puppy
KATZENFUSS: Catfeet

KIPPOHR: Soft ear
KLEIN: Small
KNOCKEN: Bones
KÖRBUCH: Studbook
KÖRZUCHT:
    Good reproductive qualities
KRUPPE: Croup
KURZ: Short
LANG: Long
LÄNGE: Length
LANGHAARIG: Long coated
MASKE (M): Mask
MUSKELN: Muscles
MUTTER: Dam
NACHSCHUB: Drive, thrust
NAGEL: Claw
NASE: Nose
OBERARM: Upper arm
OBERSCHLACHTIG: Overshot
OHREN: Ears
PFOTE: Paw
RASSE: Breed
REIN: Pure
ROT (R): Red
RIPPEN: Ribs
RUDE (R):
    Dog (as against the female)
RUND: Round
RUTE: Tail set
SATTEL (S): Saddle
SCHÄDEL: Skull
SCHEU: Shy
SCHULTER: Shoulder
SCHULTERBLATT: Shoulder-blade
SCHUSS-SCHEU: Gun-shy
SCHUSSFEST: Gun-proof
SCHWÄMMIG: Spongy
SCHWANZ: Tail
SCHWARZ: Black
SCHWARZGELB (SG): Black/gold
SCHWARZGRAU: Black/silver
SILBERGRAU: Silver/grey
STEIL: Steep

STOCKHAAR: Harsh coat
TIEF: Deep
TRABEN: Trotting
TROCKEN: Dry
UBERWINKELT: Over-angulated
UNGENÜGEND (U): Poor
UNTERSCHLACHTIG: Undershot
VATER: Sire
VEREIN: Club
VERKÄUFIG (VERK): For sale
VORDERBEINE: Forelegs
VORDERBRUST: Forechest
VORSCHUB: Reach
VORZÜGLICH: Excellent
WEICH: Soft
WEISS: White
WERFEN: Whelped
WESEN: Temperament
WESENFEST: Firm Temperament
WESENSCHEU: Shyness
WETTERFEST: Stormproof
WIDERRIST: Withers
ZOTTHAARIG: Open coated
ZUCHTBUCH: Stud book
ZUCHTBUCHNUMMER (SZ-NR):
    Stud book number
ZUCHTER: Breeder
ZUCHTPRÜFUNG:
    Approved (approval) as suit-
    able for breeding

Classification Awards made by
    German Judges:
VORZÜGLICH AUSLESE (VA):
    Excellent Selected—awarded
    only at the Hauptzuchtschau
VORZÜGLICH (V): Excellent
SEHR GUT (SG): Very Good
GUT (G): Good
AUSREICHEND (A): Satisfactory
MANGELHAFT (M): Poor
UNGENÜGEND (U): Unsatisfactory